WYLDE'S ADVENTURES IN BUSLAND

John Wylde

John Wylde

This book is dedicated to my wife, Mary, who has always encouraged me to recognise the achievements of the various enterprises described in this book.

Contents

Foreword

This work is semi-skimmed autobiography - an enthusiast and operator's **recollections** - and refers only to those aspects of my life which are relevant to my interest in public transport and my direct involvement in running buses.

Most of the photographs in part 1 and some others are my own. I am grateful to Donald Handley and Iain and Andrew Whitlam for theirs in part 2 and to my son Andrew for his in part 3. There are some others which I cannot acknowledge because the kind people who gave them to me put all the details on the back except their name, and my memory fails me.

I have included a photograph which appeared unacknowledged in Country Bus News No 6 in Spring 1958, which source is acknowledged with the caption. This photograph is of particular interest to me because it was taken at the nearest bus stop to my birthplace, probably not very long before I made my appearance.

Two photographs were taken by the 'Kentish Times' in 1963 which were used to illustrate an article in 'Passenger Transport' in 1965. I wrote to the 'Kentish Times' at their current address seeking permission to reproduce them herein but failed to receive a reply. As they clearly had no objection to their use in 1965 I cannot believe they would object now, so I have included them and acknowledged their source with the caption. I have also reproduced a letter which appeared in their correspondence column in 1968, permission to use which I sought with the request mentioned above. Perhaps the 'Kentish Times' no longer functions in the area.

Reference sources for the text are few, apart from my own inadequate memory. Principally, I found Gavin Martin's 'London Buses, 1929-1939' a valuable source of information on vehicle type codes. I have always known the difference between a 4Q4 and a 5Q5, between a 9T9 and a 10T10, and even that Tilling STLs were 8STL4, but it is a bit tricky when it comes to recognising a 1/7T7/1 at sight, and I am delighted now to know the official difference between a 2LT5 and a 2LT5/1, though I regret that my photograph of the latter variation is not up to reproduction.

Alan Lambert's book 'Hants & Sussex' contains useful information about some of the services in the Horsham area in earlier days, and confirms my feelings about the way in which some of the Traffic Commissioners discharged their responsibilities.

Innumerable people have helped me with snippets of information confirming or correcting my own recollections and records. I hope and expect to receive much more help from readers in supplying me with additional and corrected material for use in the supplement which I hope to produce in due course for students and enthusiasts who want more detailed information. Everyone knows that individuals differ in what they remember and how they remember events, and I should like the supplement to be more 3D.

Michael Calvert has provided technical advice and assistance in producing the copy for the printer, and my wife Mary has not only been involved in many of the events recorded in this book, but has helped positively in its production.

My grateful thanks are due to everybody who has contributed.

Berwick-upon-Tweed, 1998. J.D.Wylde.

LT 426 (2LT5) at Bromley Road Junction, Green Street Green, my 'home' stop, circa 1948. This style of bus architecture is my earliest recollection, and nothing will ever take its place in my affections.

PART 1.

1. 1933 to 1945. Childhood.

The London Passenger Transport Board took over responsibility for all passenger transport services in the Board's 'Special Area' except those provided by the Big Four main line railway companies, when I was seven and a half days old, on 1st July 1933.

The 'Special Area' was an area of about 20 miles radius of central London within which other operators could only provide services with the Board's consent.

Before I knew what was happening the 1934 'Balance of mileage agreement' resulted in the transfer of Country Bus routes 411 and 422 to Central Buses as routes 51 and 61 respectively. My earliest recollections are of LTs on route 51 and Leyland Cubs (Cs) on route 471. I must have only just missed remembering Dennis Darts on the latter.

I quickly learned to distinguish between the various body styles of LT but in my pre-school days that is about as far as it went.

Red ST 700 (1ST1) on loan to Country Buses at Chessington Zoo, 1948.

An interesting development just before the war was the arrival of 5Q5s on route 241, which had been extended from Sidcup to Green Street Green. I knew they weren't trolleybuses, but where was the engine? Having found it, the only place to sit was over it, of course.

Q 31, a 'Country' Q (4Q4) at Sevenoaks Bus Station. The engine is behind the off-side front wheel. The 'Central' Q (5Q5) had the entrance opposite the driver, an entirely novel idea at the time which has become universal. The wheelbase obviously had to be shortened to accommodate the door in front of the front wheels within the same overall length; this made it very manoeuvrable, but front overhang was new to bus drivers - tram drivers were used to it.

The war began when I was six years old, and the bus situation began to be a bit interesting. One morning all the buses had their blinds removed and carried small paper stickers in the bulkhead window with only the route number on. Perhaps this was when invasion was a real possibility in the summer of 1940 and the intention was the same as the removal of signposts - to make it as difficult as possible for the invaders to find their way around. After a while the restricted blind displays appeared but even as a child I remember thinking that a little more thought might have gone into the use of the space.

Being on the edge of the Central and Country areas it was interesting to note the different approach to the restricted displays. Country buses kept their separate number blinds. Later I was to learn a lot more about the different approach of the two departments to a whole range of things.

An interesting wartime development was on the LTL scooters (single-deck LTs) on route 227 where the seats were re-arranged along the sides to make more standing space. Shall we dance? I always preferred standing on buses whether there were seats vacant or not, and I **didn't** 'hold very tight please'. I got my bus legs very early on. If the conductor could keep his balance on a moving bus while taking money and issuing tickets, I certainly could.

Something I never used was the Used Tickets box. I kept my tickets and had a fine collection. When I was very small I didn't only keep my own, I picked them up off the floor as well. A conductor asked me what my mum thought about it. I replied airily that she had a Hoover. As a matter of fact the one she had, which wasn't new then, eventually went into the skip in 1997. It was a shame really, but I doubt whether even the Beamish Museum would have wanted it.

The bus services in the Orpington area were mainly of East Surrey Traction Company origin. Penfold and Brodie of Green Street Green operated a circular service via Pratts Bottom (yes, there really is somewhere called Pratts Bottom), Knockholt and Cudham which ran clockwise in the morning and anti-clockwise in the afternoon. It became route 471 and had Dennis Darts (DAs) for a short time before the C class appeared. By the time I could take an intelligent interest it was running half-hourly each way round with a joint 15-minute frequency between Green Street Green and Orpington Station.

Green Street Green had started to develop before the Green Belt Act, the Surrey Heights Light Railway proposal had not materialised, and route 471 provided the only services to Orpington Station from the village. Consequently it built up a commuter traffic which was beyond the ability of the Cubs to cope with, they being 20-seats-and-no-standing (but I travelled on one carrying 20 seated and 28 standing passengers).

London Transport's efforts to have route 471 approved for larger single decks were frustrated for many years (and rightly so). Outside the London area the traffic between Green Street Green and Orpington Station would have been dealt with by the diversion of a few journeys on route 51, but in London Transport such a solution was impossible.

For services within the Board's Special Area it was not necessary for London Transport to have a Road Service Licence, but the inflexibility of routeing sprang from the agreement with the T & G W Union. My first awareness of union power came when the single-deck route 241 was curtailed to its original route from Welling Station to Sidcup Garage (Foots Cray), and replaced between Sidcup and Green Street Green by an increase in the frequency of the double-deck route 51.

However, route 51 at that time ran from Sidcup Station to Farnborough, and the additional journeys to Green Street Green were scheduled to run through the village as route 241 had done, which was clearly in contravention of the agreement which included no joint compilation of bifurcating routes. Green Street Green instantly lost its services while Farnborough Hill enjoyed a magic carpet of empty buses until the matter was resolved. It seemed to me a curious mis-use of effort in the darkest days of the war. When order was restored, the 241-replacement services were numbered 51A, and scheduled separately.

Route 51 had not altered basically since it was transferred from Country Buses in 1934. Its progenitor, East Surrey route 2B, had continued beyond Farnborough to Bromley North Station. About a year before the formation of the L.P.T.B. East Surrey became part of London General Country Services. Either then, or earlier under the Bassom numbering system, the East Surrey route numbers were first prefixed 'S' and then the S2 and S2B became 402 and 411. Presumably East Surrey route 2A had been Sidcup to Sevenoaks, or perhaps garage workings from Sidcup to Dunton Green, but I have never come across evidence of it. If so, route 51A was its partial heir and successor somewhat belatedly.

East Surrey K 260 on route S2B at Bromley Road Junction, Green Street Green. (Unacknowledged photograph in Country Bus News No 6, Spring 1958). The driver is A.Cowley, 14746, who was still at Dunton Green in 1958, and the conductor is W.G.(Bill) Randall, who was District Superintendent (South) at Reigate when I was there.

Early in the war the Green Line services were withdrawn, and my recollection of pre-war Green Lines is slight, but I have included a photograph which I took at Windsor Castle of an original Green Line 'T' type in post-war service as a bus.

Originally built as a Green Line coach, T 219 (1/7T7/1) was photographed at Windsor Castle when in service as a bus, 1948.

During the war, petrol was severely rationed, so the comparatively small number of people who had cars could not use them much. There was full employment because of the war effort, and these two factors placed an extra burden on public transport. At the same time services were having to be trimmed. A development represented as a fuel-saving measure was the extension of fixed bus stops to the suburban and country areas where 'hail and ride' (not called that then, of course) had been the practice. Suddenly bus stop signs appeared every quarter of a mile and the travelling public had to be educated in the use of them. The principle of forming a queue when six or more people were waiting was also introduced.

Posters featuring Billy Brown of London Town were designed to educate people in rhyme. One advised people how to use the new request stops:

Face the driver, raise your hand,
You'll find that he will understand.

There was an unofficial second verse:

Of course he'll understand, the cuss,
But will he stop the flippin' bus?

This reflected the fact that buses were often full and people got used to them passing without stopping. Once my family waited for an hourly service from 11am to 4pm before we could get on.

Mention was made earlier of our only independent operator, Penfold and Brodie, whose route became 471. I never heard any comment about their attitude to the takeover of their route by the LPTB, even from Mrs Brodie, who became a regular passenger on the Orpington Rural Transport services described in a later chapter. The partners separated when the Farnborough by-pass was opened, the Brodies opening a garage and filling station on the by-pass, while the original garage at Green Street Green remained as the Penfold Coach Station. This was a very busy place at times as the feeder services came in from the surrounding area and the brown coaches left for their south coast destinations. I had to content myself with gazing in wonderment; we never actually went with them. When your father is a railwayman, you don't, do you?

2. 1945 to 1952. Teenage.

For the first couple of years after the war there was little change. The re-introduction of Green Line services was quite exciting. They had route numbers instead of the pre-war letters. Ours was 704, and ran from Tunbridge Wells to Windsor. The services were provided using the 10T10 coaches which had mostly been converted to ambulances during the war. I remember seeing one in that guise at Farnborough Hospital.

We had the added excitement of having the ex-RT 97 rebuilt as RTC 1 on route 704 for a short period. This vehicle had suffered bomb damage and was very impressive in its rebuilt form.

Supplies of practically everything seemed to be even more restricted than during the war years, so public transport was very much under pressure, and as soon as possible there were plans to improve services. By 1947 my interest was firmly on the Country Bus side.

There were two publications which appeared on bookstalls unfailingly on the first day of each month. One was the Railway Magazine, which was unfortunately beyond my reach until I started work in 1952, and the other was the Local Timetable. This extraordinary publication was a masterpiece of organisation and cost 2d per month - about one-twelfth of my pocket money - but was as vital to life as meat and drink.

About two dozen of these pocket-sized booklets covering the Country Bus area encircling London were printed and published by Index Publishers (Dunstable) Ltd, but obviously sponsored by London Transport.

In addition to **all** bus and rail services in the area they included an area map of all bus and rail routes and street maps of towns. The maps were fully comprehensive and always completely up-to-date. The area map defined the area covered by the book exactly.

The timetables were columned in movable type - not even 'linotype' as used in newspapers and books, which was not suitable for columns. Every letter, every digit, every dividing line, had to be assembled separately. Places within the area were printed in capitals and p.m. hours were in bold type. Timetables of routes running into other areas showed all services in, to and from the area concerned but not 'short journeys' wholly in other areas, for which the appropriate area book had to be consulted. It was not a matter of using the same printing forme for a route in all the areas in which it ran, therefore, but of having a different forme for each route in each area. The layout was so carefully done that there seemed to be no wasted space.

The whole set of area books, completely up-dated monthly, never inaccurate and never late, was organised by ONE MAN in an office in Victoria Street. His name was Paul Gomes (pronounced Go-mes), and it is one of the great regrets of my life that I never met him.

It was the Local Timetable for June 1947 which provided my first big post-war excitement. It showed that from the 11th of that month the Country Bus route and service patterns between Orpington and Sevenoaks were to be completely revised.

Unfortunately, this plan fell into the same trap as the 51 had some years earlier. In general, relationships between the Country Bus management and the T&GWU were a lot more amicable than those in the Central Bus department, but in this case they evidently published the timetables before agreement had been reached, and it never was. The improvements never did occur.

On 1st January 1948 the main-line railways, many minor railways, London Transport and the Tilling Group bus companies, together with Bristol Commercial Vehicles Ltd and Eastern Coachworks Ltd, became part of the British Transport Commission. Overnight, all London Transport buses had their legal lettering changed from London Passenger Transport Board to London Transport Executive.

By this time I was mid-teens, well able to explore beyond my immediate home area unaccompanied, and had friends at school with similar interests. With a fine disregard for etymology we named ourselves the Omnibusologists' Society.

Not knowing anything about the official classification of bus types other than the 'bonnet numbers', we had our own subclassification system. The first two batches of 'General' STLs had 60-seat bodies (STL1) achieved by building the top deck right out over the cab, so we naturally named them the OHTs (work it out).

STL 157 (2STL1) at Chessington Zoo, 1948. We called this type the 'OHT'. The STL1 body had 60 seats like its predecessor the Bluebird LT, but it seems to have been decided that 56 was the largest seating capacity a mobile conductor could cope with using rack tickets, so subsequent STLs had 56 seats, as did RTs. The introduction of the Gibson ticket machine enabled the first Routemasters to have 64 seats and the lengthened version 72.
***Question**: Trams and trolleybuses always had around 70 seats. Did their conductors have difficulty?*

The next (and last) batch of STLs built by the 'General', delivered in the first half of 1933, were similar except that the seating capacity was reduced to 56 and the front of the top deck was raked back (STL2), so we called them SFGs. (All right, that one is harder - *Sloping Fronted General)*. The rear profile was also slightly less straight-backed, and this became effectively the standard rear-end for all subsequent STLs except the real 'strangers in the camp'.

As the RTs appeared, it was borne in upon us that they were

rapidly displacing the more interesting older vehicles, and we adopted the practice of always selecting the oldest bus to ride on if a choice was available, a habit which is ingrained in me to this day.

STL 237 (3STL2) and Leyland Cub C 64 (2C2) at Orpington Station, 1948. This type of STL we called the 'SFG'.

A 'Tilling' STL (STL 85 - 8STL4) at Orpington Station, 1948.

The 'Tilling' STLs had petrol engines and crash gearboxes and their bodies were quite different from the 'General' and L.P.T.B. varieties. We liked them because they were different, but they must have become prohibitively expensive to maintain, as they were suddenly withdrawn. To replace them at Bromley garage (TB) for route 61 a few Leeds AEC buses were borrowed, which were mechanically similar to later STLs, with diesel engine, fluid flywheel and pre-selective gearbox.

A Leeds AEC on route 61 at Orpington, Maxwell Hotel.

To accommodate railway interests, and avoid the derision of our classical friends, the Omnibusologists' Society was re-floated as The Wheel.

Most enthusiasts are interested in vehicles rather than services, but I had one particular friend who shared my interest in services and scheduling (which our railway friends call diagramming), and I always felt that he would hardly have raised an eyebrow if a helicopter had turned up instead of a bus so long as it was on time.

Our interest was therefore satisfied to a much greater extent by studying the workings of the country buses, where scheduling was done on a garage basis rather than by individual routes.

There were many 'bits & pieces' routes in the country area, which made life more interesting for us, more difficult for the schedule compilers, and a nightmare for the crews. Works services abounded, all technically public bus services on which we could travel, and all listed in the local timetable books.

London Transport scheduling was rather more sophisticated and scientific than in most provincial companies, and the reasons for this are explored in the next chapter. We knew nothing about what went on behind the scenes, but we quickly discovered that the Local Timetable was one thing, and the Vehicle Running Schedule (VRS) was something else.

The staff were issued with District Timetables which covered several of the Local Timetable areas but contained only their own services. We felt they must contain some pretty hot information because they were headed **PRIVATE and not for publication.** These 'staff books' had to be read in conjunction with the VRS to ensure the proper operation of the services.

The VRS was the Country Bus version of what Central Buses called a Time Card. The Central Bus time card was like a timetable but instead of describing the progress of the bus down a column with the places to the left, it went horizontally, left to right, so that the timing points across the top had to be in a form of shorthand or tipped up sideways. I can think of no logical reason for doing it this way, and it is much less spatially efficient than a conventional timetable. It is also unsuited to methods of operation which involve the vehicle in more than one route, hence the need for a different system for Country Buses.

I was told that the Country Bus VRS was an adaptation of the system used by the South Eastern and Chatham Railway. It involved the use of two-letter codes which had to be unique for each terminal point, at least within the operating territory of each garage, and without adjacent garages using different codes for the same places. Code-casting had to be done carefully, therefore.

The VRS described the running of each vehicle in the garage individually, and each vehicle's VRS extract was glued onto two metal plates and varnished. One was hung on two screws in the driver's cab and the other above the faretable on the platform. The plates carried on the buses were sometimes called VRRs (Vehicle Running Records).

The method of stowage was different from the Central Bus time card. This, being more delicate, was placed in a moulded rubber holder in the driver's cab, the conductor's copy being kept with the waybill in the holder on the platform originally designed to hold the ticket rack as well.

This gave rise to a situation which can be regarded as amusing, pathetic or irritating according to taste. Apparently every bus which went to Chiswick/Aldenham for major overhaul had the screws removed and a smart new time-card holder installed. The first job of the garage engineers on receiving a bus back from overhaul was to rip out the new holder and throw it away, and re-instate the screws ready for the VRS (or VRR) plates.

I never measured these plates nor the time cards, but I cannot help feeling that they were much about the same size.

Having become so interested in the Country Bus operations I made up my mind when I was only fourteen years of age that one day I would work in the Country Bus offices at Reigate, an ambition which I am happy to say I fulfilled in due course.

The London Transport (Country Buses and Coaches) headquarters building at Reigate.

Before that, however, I turned my attention to the trams.

Everything in London is on a grander scale than anywhere else, and the London tramway system at its most extensive comprised about 300 track miles on which ran more than 2600 cars. By the beginning of the war the only trams in north London were the three routes (31,33,35) which ran through the Kingsway subway, all others having been replaced by trolleybuses.

The London United Tramways system in the south-west and the Bexley system in the south-east had been the earliest conversions to trolleybuses, but most of the south London system remained intact until 1950, when its staged closure began.

Many 'Feltham' type cars gave a further eight years useful service in Leeds after their London routes closed in 1951.

The melancholy procedure of closure went on until July 1952 and was not a 'conversion' programme like north London. This was blatant abandonment, the trams being replaced by motor buses to be closely integrated with the existing bus network.

The final day was Saturday 5th July 1952, and the official last car was met at New Cross depot in the early hours of Sunday by Lord Latham, chairman of the London Transport Executive, and driven into the depot by his deputy John Clift, an ex-tramwayman. However, it had been overlooked that there was still one car out, which arrived at New Cross just as people were dispersing from the official ceremony. There were a few enthusiasts who knew about this car, and were therefore actually the last public passengers on the London tramway system.

It had been planned originally to have the final stage three months later, but it was amalgamated with the penultimate stage, which had two results for me, one good and one very bad.

By advancing the final stage it was necessary to allocate STL type buses to route 163, replacing tram route 46, because there were not quite enough RTs yet in service. It was interesting that these last STLs were actually some of the oldest, dating from early 1933, with STL2-type bodies, or what we in the Omnibusologists' Society had dubbed SFGs.

The really bad result was that when I started work in the London Transport Schedules office in September, I was given a pass entitling me to free travel on "Central Buses, Country Buses, Trams & Trolleybuses" - but there weren't any trams! There would just have been under the original closure programme dates. There were no photocopiers then, so I was not even able to preserve the image of the pass, but had to exchange it three months later for one without the word Trams on it. My only consolation was that I could use route 163 to get to and from work and so travel on those last STLs.

There was a story about the first tramless Monday morning when an inspector was trying to pacify an impatient queue by explaining "Well, it's like this, see, a tram acts like a dredger on a queue, but a bus can only nibble at it".

38

31035

There are so many points of interest in this photograph, taken from Hungerford Bridge during the tramway abandonment programme.
1.The tram tracks on the Embankment were semi-reserved, i.e. they were paved, but road traffic was not normally allowed on them. The tram-replacement bus on route 168 was an obvious exception.
2.The Embankment routes via Westminster and Blackfriars bridges were numbered in pairs - 2/4, 16/18 etc. In almost all cases the lower number of the pair was in via Westminster and out via Blackfriars, the higher number being the opposite way round, but 36/38 were the exception. The 38 in the picture has come in over Westminster bridge and is heading out for Abbey Wood via Blackfriars.
3.Some trams were fitted with two trolleys. When the tramways in the Woolwich/Eltham area were electrified using overhead wires rather than the normal London conduit between the rails seen in the picture, pairs of wires like trolleybuses were used instead of making the earth return via the rails, for the benefit of the Royal Observatory at Greenwich. When this was no longer necessary, the second trolley was either removed or re-wired to save the conductor having to turn the trolley at the termini. The tram in the picture has two trolley bases but only one pole. Some HR2 class were not fitted with trolleys because they worked wholly on the conduit on routes 35 and 58.

The Wheel excursion to the Kent & East Sussex Railway on 6th June 1953, showing members on the resident Class O1 31065 at Headcorn. This locomotive, ancient then, has had some adventures since! The railway closed to passengers on 4th January 1954 I was on the last train, and I believe my grandfather (who had a furniture shop in Tenterden) was on the first train on the then Rother Valley Railway from Tenterden (later Rolvenden) on 2nd April 1900. You can't keep a good railway down, however, and it is open again now, of course, from Tenterden to Northiam.

The sad end of the trams at Penhall Road scrapyard, Charlton, not far from the Central Repair Works where they had been maintained.

3. 1952 to 1956. London Transport.

I started work in the London Transport bus schedules office in September 1952.

Anticipating the closure of the tramway system, the Tram & Trolleybus and Central Bus departments had been amalgamated to form Central Road Services, but the term Central Buses never died out, and I am sure the T&T staff felt that they had been taken over by, rather than amalgamated with, Central Buses.

Having previously described the difference between the Central Bus time card and the Country Bus VRS I have to admit that I never did know what the original tram time-boards were like, but the method of schedule compilation was quite different. The ex-Tram & Trolleybus compilers did not all take to the bus method like ducks to water.

The 'Tram method' had its origins in the days when tram crews had to work for up to ten hours without a break, so that there was no need to devise economical ways of providing meal breaks.

It became clear fairly early on that the same arrangements could not be applied to buses, and as bus operations increased it was realised that 'schedule efficiency' was very low, i.e. the number of crews needed to operate the buses was unnecessarily large, and the way the work was allocated was wasteful.

Very early in London Transport days, perhaps even in 'General' days, the schedules clerks were putting their minds to developing more scientific ways of compiling duty schedules, and some of the pioneers of scientific scheduling were still in the office in 1952.

When I arrived there I was put to 'learn the trade' with Jack Bunce, who had attended the same (minor public) school as myself near Eltham in south-east London.

I was very impressed with the paternalism of London Transport as an employer. Although on the salaried staff, I was paid weekly for the first four weeks, and received my first week's pay £4) on my third day at work.

After the first four weeks I was on the four-weekly cycle which resulted in 13 pay days per year, so there was never a 'long month',

3 buses Bromley (One-man operated)
+2 double decks route 61 D/S

Route 146 BROMLEY N. STN & BIGGIN HILL (BLACK HORSE)

Route 245 ORPINGTON STN & BIGGIN HILL (BLACK HORSE)

Weekdays

STAMP SHOWING **DATE** OF IMPLEMENTATION

TB	TB GAR	K	D	BG	BG	D	BN	OS	OS	K	D	BG	BG	D	BN	OS	OS	BN	D	BG	BG	D	BN	OS
1	5.51	6.1	6.13	6.30	6.38	6.52		7.14	7.17		7.38	7.55	8.1	8.15	8.43			8.45	9.13	9.30	9.38	9.52		10.14
4	6.18	28	40			6.42	7.10	To Route 61 7.20																
2	7.43									7.53	8.4	8.21→	23	37		8.59	9.17		38	55	10.1	10.15	10.43	
14	7.18	7.28	7.40			7.42	8.10	To Route 61 8.16																
3	6.51	7.1	7.13	7.30	7.38	7.52		8.14	8.17		38	55	9.1	9.15	9.43			9.45	10.13	10.30	38	52		11.14

	BG	D	K	BN/D	OS/K	TB GAR/BN	TB GAR	
→	32	17*‡	15*	16	2		1	→ } = xxx miles
←	32	17*‡	14‡	16	3*		–	← } = xxx miles

* + 1 jny by TB 4 Route 61 D/S
\+ 1 jny by TB 14 Route 61 D/S
‡ + 1 jny by TB 14 Route 61 D/S

Running times

Bromley N. Stn - Biggin Hill 42 mins
Orpington Stn - Biggin Hill 35 mins

Bus Spreadover

TB	
1	17.47
2	15.17
3	15.46
	48.50

DESTINATION EQUIPMENT REQUIRED		
ROUTE	DESTINATION	VIA
146	BROMLEY NORTH STATION	DOWNE KESTON
"	BIGGIN HILL (BLACK HORSE)	KESTON DOWNE
"	DOWNE	KESTON
245	ORPINGTON STATION	DOWNE
"	BIGGIN HILL (BLACK HORSE)	DOWNE

Times at Orpington Station to be maintained for connections with trains

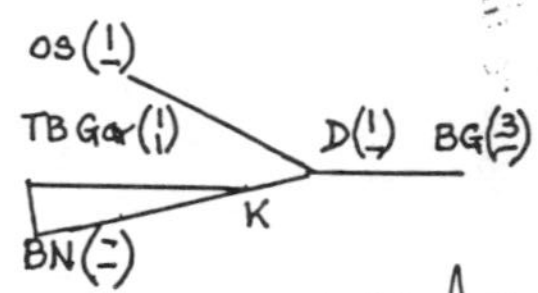

BN Bromley North Stn
K Keston The Fox
D Downe High Street
BG Biggin Hill Black Horse
OS Orpington Station

Compiled by J.D.W. Written by J.D.W

22

Ten years before the ORTA proposals were made, I wrote this fantasy schedule in the Central Bus style. It has features which were very unusual in Central Buses, though common in Country Buses:
1. The three buses used for the main services were to be
(a) one-man operated, (b) jazzed between the two routes 146/245;
2. Two route 61 double decks were to be used to provide supplementary peak services.
To accommodate any, let alone all, of these features in Central Buses would have required a Special Agreement with the T&GWU.
The time schedule (only the morning peak period leading into the midday off-peak is shown) was written in black from Biggin Hill, and red towards Biggin Hill.
To comply with the route numbering system in force at the time, route 146 would probably have had to be renumbered with a 200-series number to indicate a single-deck route, although there were one or two new double-deck routes which had been given 200-series numbers, e.g. route 229.
On the route diagram, the terminal working allowances are shown in parenthesis (e.g. BG 3 minutes in, nil out). In Central Buses, these had to be added to the running time to define the arrival/departure times. The minimum layover time was normally two minutes, which assumed crew operation. More would have been allocated for one-man operation, for which there was little precedent.
In Country Buses, the terminal working would have been carried out within the layover time between arrival and departure according to the agreed running time. The minimum layover time was three minutes for crew operation and five for one-man. Timing tests were always carried out on Tuesdays, and the real test was to see how slowly the driver of the bus being followed could manage to drive without being accused by the management of 'scratching'.

but it played havoc with monthly standing orders at the bank for those few who had such things. Every fourth Wednesday we went to the Cashier's office and I drew my £16, regarding Jack, who had been there for five years, as 'passing rich' with his £29.

We worked a 38-hour week. Each Tuesday we worked an extra hour and had every third Saturday morning off. At this time the road staff were still working a 44-hour six-day week for about £5.

In the spring of 1953 I was offered the chance to fulfil my ambition of working in the Country Bus offices at Reigate. I was still officially located at 55 Broadway so the bulk of the time spent travelling to and from Reigate was within my normal working day, and I travelled on railway warrants, so I was blissfully happy.

An added benefit was that I would have been at work for such a short time on Saturday mornings that it was decided by the management that I should simply have every Saturday off.

The Country Bus schedules office was a small, friendly office with about a dozen staff, smaller than just one section of the Central Bus office. The schedules looked deceptively simple compared with the route 607 trolleybus schedule which I had written-up, with 70 buses per hour. Country Buses only had about 1000 vehicles compared with 10,000 Central buses and trolleybuses. The schedules were not as simple as they looked, with buses flitting from route to route.

My job was to go through the schedules and apportion all the scheduled time to the various routes worked, so that a cost per mile figure could be calculated for each route, rather than having only a cpm for the garage as a whole. This was 20 years before the National Bus Company produced the Beetham Formula for Operational Costing, but there were at this stage serious misgivings, in London Transport Country Buses at least, about the average cost per mile being the only figure available to compare with revenue per mile as the test of profitability. The principle of marginal costing was acknowledged, but regarded (rightly) as far too dangerous to be used without a very clear arrangement for covering the overhead costs, with which London Transport was weighed down to a far greater extent than any other operator.

This burden became clear when I visited Reigate soon after Country Buses had been transferred from London Transport to the National Bus Company in 1970. I found staff overwhelmed with enormous piles of documents sent down from 'up the road', and was greeted with "Oh, John, we had **no** idea what they did for us at Broadway until we had to do it for ourselves!".

I returned to Broadway for the winter of 1953-54, and on 31st May 1954 I took up a vacancy for a Class 'B' woman clerk, which was the lowest clerical grade, in the office of the Divisional Superintendent (South), Country Buses & Coaches, at Reigate. I knew when I was in the schedules office that it was a very specialised job, and I wanted some broader experience. I took the job at Reigate rather than one in Central Road Services because of my interest in the Country area.

The journey from Orpington to Reigate by public transport was not straightforward, but the reliability was fantastic. The railway (Southern Region) and Country Buses were virtually always spot on.

I could save a lot of changing trains by using Central Bus route 54 from Beckenham to East Croydon, and on paper the timing was perfect. In practice it became a non-option because the route 54 bus almost always ran early, so I usually ended up changing at Beckenham, Crystal Palace, Norwood Junction and East Croydon, which generally worked like clockwork.

The most interesting job I had while in the Divisional Office was on Derby Day. Country Buses ran two special routes to the racecourse, 406E and 406F from Epsom railway station and town centre, the former being a really intensive operation.

Buses were brought from every South Division garage to do their bit. How many trips they could do depended on how far they had come, to keep within the agreed duty hours. The L.T. agreement got nowhere near the legal limits, the Executive being very much in the grip of the T&GWU, but relations were more cordial in the Country area than the Central.

The Assistant Divisional Superintendent was Jack Wooler-with-one-L (as he described himself), at 39 years old the youngest Senior

Executive Assistant in London Transport. (A few years later posts at this grade were being filled by young men straight from University). On hearing of a difficulty with one of the drivers, Jack enquired what was the problem. "The union says I only have to do fourteen trips, and I've done them" he said. Jack replied "Well, get down out of that cab and go and get your money from the union". We all held our breath. The driver did a fifteenth trip and we all breathed again. In Central Buses an incident like that would probably have brought the whole of London Transport to a standstill within a few hours.

To prepare for slick crew changes at Epsom there was an inspector in Chalk Lane with a walkie-talkie who reported the running numbers of the buses passing him to the control van, where I kept a list from which another inspector identified the crews needed and went to fetch them from the canteen.

I have no personal recollection of the following scurrilous rumour, which has the ring of truth about it. The story goes that the Epsom special services were all crewed by rest day working, but the buses were drawn from the Special Events Fleet, normally kept unlicenced in back yards for use on occasions such as this, and the Ministry of Transport Vehicle Examiners had to be given days off to 'go to the races' **off duty** for fear that if they were on duty anywhere in the area on race days they would be bound to act on what they saw. It would be nice to see this rumour denied so that we could be certain of its truth. It has been said you should never believe anything until it has been officially denied.

After about a year I developed a skin rash which the doctor put down to nervous strain arising from my long travelling, so I reluctantly applied for a transfer back to Broadway. While awaiting this I bought a B.S.A. Bantam 125cc motor cycle and cut my travelling time in half. It was incredibly economical and I was fully protected against rain, but when the weather became cold I had to give it up.

My last posting in London Transport was at Broadway in the office of the Traffic Superintendent (Central Road Services). I was a link in the chain of investigation of public complaints about

Central Buses, such as when a passenger wrote or phoned to say he had waited for three-quarters of an hour for a bus on a route with a scheduled 15-minute frequency, for example.

On receipt of a complaint, the Public Relations Officer's staff acknowledged it and sent a memo to our office. We then sent a memo to the appropriate Divisional Office, who in turn sent a memo to the relevant District Office, who took it up with the operating garage. The garage staff then checked the running records for the day in question.

At each stage the staff had to work through the accumulated incoming memos methodically, dictate their outgoing memo, await its return from the typing pool and forward it to the authorised signatory for despatch. Thus by the time the garage staff received the complaint it usually referred to a day several weeks earlier. They then replied to their District office, usually to the effect that they could find no record of any such gap in service on that route at that place and time on the day in question. The reply was then transmitted, office by office, typing pool by typing pool, authorised signatory by authorised signatory, through the system until at last the P.R.O. had the unenviable task of replying to the complainant to the effect that he must be either a fool or a liar.

The complainant, meanwhile, owing to the belated reply, had probably forgotten all about the incident, having made the complaint about it in the heat of anger. The reply usually re-kindled the anger and set up a 'Who are you calling a liar?' exchange, which sometimes meant a re-investigation. The next reply from the P.R.O. was probably signed by a different authorised signatory, and habitual correspondents could point to perhaps half-a-dozen examples of letters all ostensibly signed by the P.R.O. but all obviously in different hands, thus re-inforcing the idea that they were being made to look foolish.

Not being able to stand this, I went to a teacher-training college.

4. Before we proceed.

The remainder of this book is an account of my experiences as an operator. I shall welcome anecdotes and different views of events, to be incorporated at a later date in a 'warts and all' supplement which will be more suited to students than to the general reader.

Nothing succeeds like success. In our society success is measured in financial terms. A business which is a financial success is credited with other qualities such as being a good employer and giving its customers good service, and vice-versa.

Transport is not an end in itself, it is a means to an end. Its purpose is to satisfy the demand for the movement of people and goods. To do this it requires vehicles (and the resources with which to maintain them), and staff to operate them.

Bus companies are run by three people who take different views of their function. The engineer thinks that the buses are for him to play with, to take to bits and put together again. The accountant has the curious idea that they ought to make a profit. The traffic manager believes that their purpose is to carry passengers.

I am not an engineer, so I want buses that never go wrong, and never have to be in the garage. I am not an accountant, but I want financial results which will be adequate to support the services which I, as a traffic manager, must operate to meet the demands of the passengers without whom we would have no function.

I am a pioneer. Many of the things I do have never been done before. My friends in the big undertakings laughed when I was the first to run minibuses on regular local services, many years before anything of the sort happened in Exeter. Later, when it became fashionable, they all did it themselves, but with other people's money (yours).

My businesses have succeeded in pioneering new methods of meeting the needs of people for public transport services in circumstances where they might not otherwise have had any. The engineers have done well: they have come to work, done their job,

taken their money and gone home. Accountants, like lawyers, win irrespective of the success or failure of their clients.

Viewed with the objectivity of accountants, my businesses have never achieved on-going viability because they have all been entrepreneurial, and lacked the sound unimaginative base which characterises most bus companies. Much of the failure has been due to doing the right thing at the wrong time, so that my successors have sometimes managed to ride the surf that overwhelmed me.

Hindsight being an exact science, I can say with the knowledge I have now but did not have at the time, that some of my recommendations and actions would have been different had I been abl to foresee later developments. Suffice it to say that everything was done in good faith on the basis that 'it seemed like a good idea at the time'.

This work takes a positive view of events, to place on record the part played in the development of public transport services in three rural areas, much of which has had a lasting effect, and has therefore achieved considerable success in improving the quality of life for people in those areas.

There are one or two references to suppressed and latent demand. Suppressed demand is that which exists but is frustrated by the lack of the means to satisfy it, while latent demand is that which is created by the provision of the means to satisfy it.

I have been rather sparing in references to individuals because it would be impossible to mention everybody who has been involved in the story which unfolds in parts 2 & 3. Personal references are therefore generally restricted to those which are essential to the plot.

PART 2

1. The Orpington area.

Underlying the London clay is a layer of chalk which rises to form the Chiltern hills to the north of London, and the North Downs to the south. The Downs extend from the celebrated White Cliffs of Dover to the almost equally famous Hog's Back west of Guildford. They achieve a height of barely 300 metres, but are nevertheless a notable feature of the landscape of south-east England.

In the vicinity of the point where the London Borough of Bromley meets the counties of Kent and Surrey lies Biggin Hill, well known for its Royal Air Force fighter base whose importance reached its peak in the Battle of Britain.

The drainage pattern on the dip-slope of the North Downs is identified by the dry valleys which fall northward to the points where they meet the clay and gravels. The water in the porous chalk is forced to the surface at places such as Orpington ponds and becomes a small river, in this case the river Cray. At times when the water table in the chalk was high, the source of the river Cray used to back up to the pond at Green Street Green (under the present roundabout), the section between Green Street Green and Orpington being a typical winterbourne.

The river Cray was reputedly navigable for small craft such as dinghies and punts, but never had any commercial potential as a navigation.

The principal industry in the Cray valley was papermaking, which was undertaken at two or three sites using water power. Market gardening, established earlier, developed when the railways were built and enabled the produce to be conveyed to London more quickly.

The Tonbridge Direct line of the South Eastern Railway, which was opened throughout in April 1868, passed through Orpington. This stimulated its growth, at first as a recreational centre with golf courses and a special promotion to encourage rambling based on railway stations. This was done through a series of guides by 'Walker Miles' sponsored by the railway companies, in this case the S.E.R. The author was Edmund Sefang Taylor, who died in 1904 and is buried in Godstone churchyard.

Before the electrification of the railway in 1926 there was a slow growth in the 'adventitious' population - those who chose to reside in the area but work in London. Orpington was still a village rather than a town, with a population of less than 5000, little industry other than agriculture, one or two country houses and a few shops (one occupied by my mother's family having moved from Tenterden). The 'main' road ran along the Cray valley from Sidcup, joining the Hastings road (A21) at the north end of Green Street Green village at what was known as the Bromley Road junction. There were lanes from Green Street Green to villages on the downs, one of the more notable of these being Downe (sic), where Charles Darwin occupied Down House (sic) and wrote his 'Origin of Species'.

The electrification of the railway resulted in a rapid growth of population as the Orpington area (and everywhere of similar characteristics) developed into the southern equivalent of Metroland. The Cray valley attracted light industry when a by-pass road was built avoiding the villages. Some well-known names became associated with the area, such as Crittal Windows and Morphy-Richards.

The Green Belt (London and Home Counties) Act 1938 halted building development other than for 'infill' in the areas already developed. The built-up area thus came to a very abrupt halt on the southern outskirts of Orpington, leaving the villages of Chelsfield, Green Street Green and Farnborough almost untouched, but within sight of the new suburbia.

In the twenties many unsubstantial dwellings were built at Biggin Hill on quite large plots which had been bought for as little as £20 per acre, often by ex-servicemen using their gratuities. This resulted in the area becoming a most unprepossessing shanty town for some years.

DATED THIS 7TH DAY OF AUGUST, 1928.

THE PROMOTERS

OF

THE SOUTHERN HEIGHTS
LIGHT RAILWAY COMPANY

AND

THE
SOUTHERN RAILWAY COMPANY.

Working Agreement.

SCHEDULE.

STATIONS OR HALTS WITH THEIR MILEAGE FROM THE COMMENCEMENT OF THE RAILWAY AT ORPINGTON.

WESTERHAM HILL	6m. 11chns.
TATSFIELD	8m. 9chns.
HAMSEY GREEN	12m. 56chns.
CHELSHAM FOR WARLINGHAM	11m. 44chns.
GREEN STREET GREEN FOR FARNBOROUGH	1m. 7chns.
DOWNE AND KESTON	3m. 5chns.
CUDHAM AND BIGGIN HILL	5m. 14chns.
MITCHLEY WOOD	14m. 12chns.

On 7th August 1928 a Working Agreement was signed between the Southern Heights Light Railway Company and the Southern Railway Company for the construction and operation of a line connecting Orpington and Sanderstead via Green Street Green, Downe, Biggin Hill, Tatsfield and Warlingham. Colonel Holman Fred Stephens was one of the promoters. The headquarters of the Colonel Stephens railways, which included the Kent & East Sussex, was at Tonbridge. The agreement provided for the Southern to operate the line, which it would no doubt have done as part of its growing suburban electrified network, probably by extension of the Mid-Kent line trains terminating at Sanderstead. The Mid-Kent line ran through the eastern outskirts of Croydon, with stations at Coombe Road and Bingham Road. There was a short branch from the north into a terminal station at Addiscombe.

It is probably fair to speculate that if the SHLR had been built, Bingham Road station would have been developed and Addiscombe closed.

The Working Agreement contained a schedule of stations to be built on the SHLR, with their distances from Orpington, but the order appears to be entirely random, being neither geographical nor alphabetical.

The political preparation for the 1938 Green Belt Act was already gathering momentum. In December 1929 the First Report of the Greater London Regional Planning Committee was published. I have not been able to confirm what seems plausible, that the Greater London Region as defined became the London Transport Special Area. It certainly went further out than the Greater London we came to know in 1965, with which the London Transport Special Area became contiguous in 1970, when the Country Bus department was transferred to the National Bus Company.

It seems likely that pressure was put on the promoters of the railway not to proceed. Had it been built, and the prospect of the Green Belt not stopped development, the character of the area would have been vastly different by the beginning of the war.

The probable route of the Southern Heights Light Railway

In 1934 the Bromley Rural District Council was replaced by the Orpington Urban District Council as the local authority for the area. In the fifties it was accepted that Biggin Hill was a special case, and a development programme was approved to open up the Valley with high-density modern housing. The Orpington Urban District Act, 1954, required that the roads had to be made before the houses were built, but unfortunately it did not require that the access roads to them should be improved. Construction went ahead, with the only access for construction traffic being two steep and narrow lanes - Stock Hill, on which it was just possible for two cars to pass with care, and Polesteeple Hill, on which it was not.

I saw a heavily-laden brick lorry descending Polesteeple Hill with the driver periodically applying the brakes, but the only difference that made was whether the wheels were going round or not.

During the process of construction the Orpington Urban District became part of the London Borough of Bromley (April 1965).

The lanes through the valley led to New Addington to the north-west and Tatsfield to the south-west. New Addington is a large over-spill estate in the London Borough of Croydon, and has always presented London Transport with enormous difficulties in catering for the peak traffic. Hopefully the construction of the tramway (pending at the time of writing) will solve a very long-standing problem. Remember what the inspector said in 1952!

2. The Orpington Rural Transport Association.

In 1961 the Chairman of the Orpington U.D.C. was Alfred Howard, also a Kent County Councillor, whose ward was part of Biggin Hill. He was concerned that there had never been a public transport link between Biggin Hill and Orpington. In 1934 the U.D.C. had taken over the offices at Orpington as well as the responsibilities of the Bromley R.D.C., so it was not a question of Biggin Hill having become isolated because of the change. If the Southern Heights Light Railway had been built, it would have created the link in the thirties.

To make the journey by bus meant a walk of more than half a mile between two services of different frequencies, and the seven mile journey often took more than an hour.

A narrow, winding lane connected Biggin Hill with Downe, about half way to Orpington, and there was ribbon development along this lane, particularly in the Berrys Green area. According to London Transport's accessibility criteria, Berrys Green was officially unserved by public transport.

Orpington U.D.C. had a majority of Liberal councillors, and there was a common interest in accessibility to Orpington on the part of those representing the wards comprising Biggin Hill, Berrys Green and Downe. The member for Downe was Eric Lubbock, who was elected Member of Parliament for the Orpington constituency in 1962, and is now Lord Avebury.

Alfred Howard and my father were both deacons of the Baptist church in Orpington, and one day there was a meeting in our house. After the meeting, Alfred, knowing that I had worked for London Transport, asked me what chance there was of persuading L.T. to start the desired bus service. I said there was no chance of L.T. doing it, but I would. It would have to be a minibus because of the roads, and L.T. would have to consent to it because of their inability to do it themselves.

After some consideration, over which the 1962 election took precedence, the Orpington Rural Transport Association was formed. The members were Eric Lubbock M.P. (President), Alfred

Howard, C.C., J.P., (Chairman), Wilfrid Ashworth, Michael Edwardes-Evans, and Philip Golding. Mrs Pat Langford was secretary, and I was embryo manager. The object was to get a bus service from the wards they represented to Orpington, even if the Association had to do it itself. It was felt that the best way to concentrate London Transport's mind was to apply for consent for the Association to operate a service.

The lanes which formed the only route linking Biggin Hill, Berrys Green and Downe were subject to a restriction banning vehicles with more than 15 seats. This included the driver, so the maximum permitted seated payload was therefore 14. The smallest London Transport vehicles at this time were the GS type with 26 seats, which had replaced the 20-seat Leyland Cubs in October 1953.

London Transport regarded routes operated with GSs as non-viable ipso-facto, so there was no possibility of it considering the use of a vehicle only half the size. It would normally have sought removal of the size restriction if it really wanted to provide a service, but this would have been so obviously impracticable, and in any case L.T. was certain that the route would be 'unremunerative' with any size of vehicle.

ROUTE

479 to ORPINGTON via Leaves Green and Shire Lane

Saturday only

	am	am	pm	pm			
Biggin Hill *Post Office*	9 34	10 46	1 35	2 47	...	...	...
Leaves Green *Kings Arms*	9 42	10 54	1 43	2 55	..	..	..
Keston Church *Downe Road*	9 46	10 58	1 47	2 59	...	...	...
Sevenoaks Road *Farnborough Hill*	9 56	11 8	1 57	3 9	..	..	..
Orpington Station	10 5	11 17	2 6	3 18	...	...	...

ROUTE

479 to BIGGIN HILL Post Office

via Shire Lane and Leaves Green

Saturday only

	am	pm	pm	pm			
Orpington Station	10 10	12 33	2 11	4 11	...	...	...
Sevenoaks Road *Farnborough Hill*	10 19	12 42	2 20	4 20	..	..	..
Keston Church *Downe Road*	10 29	12 52	2 30	4 30	...	...	...
Leaves Green *Kings Arms*	10 33	12 56	2 34	4 34	..	..	..
Biggin Hill *Post Office*	10 41	1 4	2 42	4 42	...	...	...

NOTE—This timetable does not necessarily apply on Bank Holidays. While every effort will be made to keep to the timetables, London Transport does not undertake that its buses will be operated in accordance with them, or at all. London Transport will not be responsible for any loss, damage or inconvenience caused by reason of any operating failure or in consequence of any inaccuracies in the timetables.

LONDON TRANSPORT, 55 BROADWAY, S.W.1. ABBey 1234 **16.2.63**

163/50Z/350(75) 991 Kelly & Kelly Ltd, London

It should be appreciated by the present-day reader, who has been familiar with minibuses on local services for many years, that at this time they were typically very basic van conversions, having little headroom, access normally by the rear doors, and usually longitudinal, often wooden-slatted, seats along the sides. The Public Service Vehicle Construction & Use Regulations had been modified in 1956 to permit such vehicles to be given a Certificate of Fitness, and therefore a P.S.V. licence, but it was generally accepted that they would only be used for workmen's transport and youth club outings. The purpose of the relaxed standards was to legalise and therefore control the growing use of these vehicles for such activities.

London Transport's reaction to the Association's request for consent to operate the route with service only on Saturdays was to say that it believed there was no need for a service from Biggin Hill to Orpington, but if there was then it should provide it.

Route 479 began operation on Saturday 16th February 1963 with four services each way at irregular intervals. A duplicate bus was required for the last service from Orpington on the first day.

The route was the best compromise that L.T. could devise between what the Association wanted and what it could provide. This was from Biggin Hill as routes 410 & 705 to Keston church, then via the unpopulated Shire Lane to Green Street Green, then as route 471 to Orpington station. The journey time was 31 minutes.

It did not run via Berrys Green and Downe, however, so it failed to benefit the people who were unserved by public transport according to London Transport's own criteria, whose needs were a fundamental part of the Association's case. In fact, the main traffic it could be expected to raise to satisfy suppressed and latent demand was what it could abstract from routes 410 and 705, with a very small consequential effect on route 61. It was well used on the first day as a novelty, but thereafter it wholly justified L.T.'s scepticism about its potential viability, and it was withdrawn after four months.

Route 479 had been introduced in response to the O.R.T.A.'s request for consent to operate a service, and we knew that it was most unlikely to be successful in the form which it took. We asked London Transport to give us adequate notice of any intention to withdraw it so that the Association could re-submit its application for consent. That request was ignored, and the first we knew of the withdrawal was the statutory one-week's notice it was required to give the passengers.

Following its withdrawal, London Transport granted consent for the Association to provide the service, and an 'unforeseen' Road Service Licence was granted to continue operation with the minimum of alteration, and without a break, from 22nd June 1963. The only route modification was to use the up-side approach road at Orpington station, which we had all to ourselves, rather than the down-side used by all the terminating L.T. services. A later service from Orpington was included in the timetable.

A Bedford CA minibus was hired from George Bowser (Westerham Coaches), which was normally driven by his wife with me acting as conductor. We had been told (incorrectly) by the Metropolitan Traffic Area office that a conductor had to be carried, but it enabled me to assist the passengers in boarding and alighting through the rear door and to assess the traffic.

We soon had a small band of volunteer conductors. One of these, Mr W.H.E.Wayman, lived in the Valley and was of a different political persuasion from the members of the Association, but he threw himself into the arrangements with the greatest enthusiasm because he saw that it was a genuine community venture and not a political gimmick. Another was Roy Edwards, who found that he became queasy on the minibus, but his interest remained and he became a Principal in a subsequent venture described in a later chapter.

The other three volunteers - Colin Davis, Ken Payne and Ken Kitney, who all had highly-paid responsible jobs but were tickled pink to be bus conductors on Saturdays - lost no time in getting their P.S.V. driving licences in the autumn. In preparation for ORTA having its own vehicle, George Bowser had very kindly allowed me to take my test on his minibus in the summer.

Although the term was not in use, nor was the concept

understood in 1963, we had set up what was probably the first Community Bus Scheme.

ORTA's application to re-route via Berrys Green and Downe was granted and took effect on 27th July 1963. There was no traffic to and from Orpington railway station, and B.R. charged sixpence per departure for the use of the approach road, so the revised services terminated at the War Memorial stop in Sevenoaks road, from which they departed for the return journey via the roundabout. The number of journeys was increased to six.

In August we were informed by a very apologetic member of the Traffic Area staff that we had been misinformed about the need for a conductor, which was not required on small vehicles. He need not have worried, because Mr Wayman at least was so enthusiastic that he insisted on continuing with his duties until the increase in traffic meant that there was no room for him.

Fares were developed naturally from the London Transport fares on route 479, and were broadly controlled by L.T. as part of its consent to operate.

Rack tickets were used at first, two unserviced punches being bought from London Transport for five shillings each; I cannot remember how the racks were obtained, but some of them were rather larger than L.T. had used. Tickets were printed by John Russell, who had been a staunch supporter of 'The Wheel' at school, and printed souvenir tickets for special occasions.

The importance of providing information was recognised. It is difficult to understand now why it was accepted in those days that bus timetables had to be bought, they were not free. The first ORTA timetable leaflets were priced at one penny, later ones twopence, the whole of which the agents kept as 100% commission on sales. They often just gave them away. Freely available information was a concept which had not quite arrived, but we hastened it!

At the principal stopping places we attached to whatever trees or posts were convenient, simple red-painted boards about a foot square onto which were glued white poster timetables. At first

The Orpington Rural Transport Association's own Austin minibus takes over from the Bedford hired from Westerham Coaches.

Mr W .H. E. Wayman issues a ticket to the President, Mr Eric Lubbock M.P. (now Lord Avebury), watched by the Chairman, Cllr Alfred Howard, C.C., J.P., and the author.

(Photographs by KENTISH TIMES).

these were boldly under-printed with large red BUS STOP wording. Later the BUS STOP sign was printed in black on separate Dayglo orange slips. The timetables were easier to read without the under-printing. The boards were then varnished. Vandalism and graffiti were not a problem.

Consideration now had to be given to obtaining a vehicle of our own. It may be of interest to present-day readers to know that the word 'minibus' was not then in general use. The British Motor Corporation J2 van was built by both Austin and Morris. The passenger versions were called the Austin Omnicoach and the Morris Minibus. It was the name of the Morris version which caught on and came to be applied to all passenger-carrying vehicles which were bigger than a car but not as big as a 'proper' bus.

In August I traded-in my mini-van as a 50% deposit on an Austin J2 Omnicoach. It had 11 side-facing seats and a side loading door. The front seat was not certified for passenger use and the door was marked 'Courier only' - just right for Mr Wayman. In fact, he had accepted that his role was now outgrown, and the front seat was removed and the space used for luggage. The Association paid the balance so that it would be used as the bus on Saturdays and my own transport at other times.

I was personally only available on alternate Saturdays, so until the first volunteers were licenced in October, a Trojan P3 minibus was hired with driver from Thames-Weald of West Kingsdown. This firm was already operating a minibus service through the North Downs between Dartford and Sevenoaks, and was run by a psychiatrist, Dr Heffernan. It was not a community bus service like ours, because it did not involve the local community in its operation, nor could the route justify much development, although it was later extended at both ends, at first through the Dartford Tunnel to Romford and then in the other direction to Gatwick Airport.

An unexpected difficulty was that of insuring the minibus. The reaction of most insurers was emphatically negative, but eventually the risk was covered, subject to some quite extraordinary conditions such as the route not entering a town (not defined) and specifically

ORPINGTON RURAL TRANSPORT

BUS STOP

BIGGIN HILL AND ORPINGTON

BOARDING & ALIGHTING RESTRICTIONS:
Towards Orpington, no passenger may be set down before Old Tye Avenue or picked up after High Elms
Towards Biggin Hill, no passenger may be set down before High Elms or picked up after Old Tye Avenue

From 1st September, 1964.

	TUESDAYS WEDNESDAYS FRIDAYS & SATURDAYS			EVENING JOURNEYS WEDNESDAYS & SATURDAYS ONLY		
Orpington Stn., Crofton Road		11.58	3.58	5.58	7.58R	10.38R
Orpington Memorial, Station Rd.	9.00	12.00	4.00	6.00	8.00R	10.40R
Green St Green, Glentrammon Rd.	9.04	12.04	4.04	6.04	8.04R	10.44R
Downe, Forgecroft	9.12	12.12	4.12	6.12	8.12R	10.52R
Berrys Green, Post Office	9.18	12.18	4.18	6.18	8.18R	10.58R
Biggin Hill, Haig Road	9.24	12.24	4.24	6.24	8.24R	11.04R
Biggin Hill, Post Office	9.36	1.36	4.36	6.36		
Berrys Green, Post Office	9.42	1.42	4.42	6.42		
Downe, Forgecroft	9.48	1.48	4.48	6.48		
Green Street Green	9.56	1.56	4.56	6.56		
Orpington Memorial	10.00	2.00	5.00	7.00		
Orpington Station	10.02	2.02	5.02	7.02		

R = Runs for Return-ticket holders only.

LEAFLETS containing a complete list of stopping places, as well as times, may be obtained free from the driver or agents:
ORPINGTON—Central Wool Shop.
DOWNE—Post Office Stores.
BERRYS GREEN—Mrs. Miles, 7 Bertrey Cottages
BIGGIN HILL—Post Office & Builders' Supply

TO HIRE THE BUS 'phone Orpington 21636.

excluding express carriage operation. This had to be altered when we were asked to provide a short service in Orpington for schoolchildren which needed to be licenced as an Express Carriage.

The route via Berrys Green and Downe proved the social justification for the Association's efforts. The number of services had to be increased to meet the demand, and there was pressure for service during the week. It became obvious that the idea of a simple service which I could provide personally with some volunteer assistance would require reassessment.

The author arriving at Berrys Green on a short-working from Biggin Hill with the 11-seat Austin, NPV 828.

The Association had to consider how it would respond to the demand for service during the week. Apart from the fear that extra services might simply spread the existing traffic more thinly and jeopardise the viability of the whole operation, there was the practical difficulty of staffing them.

It was felt that Monday was still 'washing day', Thursday was early-closing day in Orpington, and Friday was too close to Saturday, so it had to be either Tuesday or Wednesday. Tuesday was chosen.

All the Saturday drivers were in full-time employment, so two housewives, Yvonne White, who had driven ambulances during the war, and Molly Sinclair, joined the panel of volunteer drivers to cover the services on Tuesdays. A token payment was made to cover their expenses, but there was a strong community service element in their willingness to take part in this venture.

It soon became apparent that demand on Tuesdays was heavier than on Saturdays and less flexible. The growing demand on Saturdays had been successfully met by increasing the number of services, but this ploy was not so successful on Tuesdays. Housewives needed to travel while their children were in school, so earlier and later services were of no use to them. It meant that activity would have to spread to other days in the week. From 1st September 1964 services ran on Tuesdays, Wednesdays, Fridays and Saturdays.

The Association was fortunate that the Austin minibus was outstandingly reliable, but with the expansion of the timetable it was considered prudent to acquire a second vehicle. In August 1964 a 13-seat Trojan P4 was purchased. It was a coach-built small bus rather than a converted van, although a van version was available. Trojans were built individually because there were so few of them. They were made in Croydon.

The 13-seat Trojan, YBY 214. When it was good, it was very, very good......

In order to satisfy the ground clearance requirement of the P.S.V. Construction & Use Regulations, the front axle as fitted to the van could not be used on the bus. The stub axles and steering gear were bolted directly to the chassis, and the bolts had an alarming tendency to shear. The engine was the Perkins four-cylinder diesel (the P3 mentioned earlier had a three-cylinder engine). The Austin had a petrol engine, but both vehicles returned about 25 miles per gallon.

When the Trojan was added to the fleet, the ticket-issuing system was partly modernised by hiring 5-unit Ultimate machines from Bell Punch. Tickets could be issued either singly or in pairs, making ten values available. There were meters to record the number of double-issues. Traffic audit was a headache! Racks were retained for return tickets.

The additional days of operation would have placed too heavy a burden on the two lady drivers. It was decided to employ a driver during the week, leaving Saturdays to be covered by the volunteers. It was thought that the job might suit a retired bus driver, and the advertisement coincided with the retirement of Tom White from Sidcup L.T. garage.

Tom had been for many years Chairman of the Central Bus Committee of the Transport & General Workers' Union. As such, he had probably done very little actual bus driving, and he entered into the spirit of our organisation in a way which surprised and delighted us. To provide back-up in case of sickness he introduced another retired driver living locally, 'Barney' Gay.

There were some incidents which sum up Tom's attitude. First, when he arrived for interview the red Trojan was standing outside. Tom walked round it, sighed, and said "Is this the bus? Well, at least it's the right colour". The Austin was two-tone grey and looked less obviously bus-like. One morning, Tom approached two people waiting by the side of the road, so he stopped but they made no move. "Are you waiting for the bus?" he enquired. "Yes" they replied. "Well, come on, then" he said. "Is **this** the bus?" they asked. Tom was exasperated and said "What do you think it is, a sausage machine?"

On another occasion Tom arrived at Berrys Green to find two regular passengers just getting into a van. Tom bellowed at the driver "That's my living you're taking away, son". The two 'regulars' climbed out and sheepishly paid their fares on the bus.

Later, when we were running a business service for journeys to and from work on Mondays to Fridays, but no 'off-peak' services on Mondays or Thursdays (from 5th October 1964), another of the 'regulars' said to Tom one Wednesday morning "If I'm not on the first bus tomorrow, I'll be on the second". "Right-ho" said Tom, and then thought 'The second bus doesn't run on Thursdays', so when the passenger was not on the first bus the following day, Tom parked the bus after the first trip and went back to Biggin Hill in his car for the passenger.

From 22nd March 1965 a full Monday to Friday timetable was operated, but after some experience it was decided to delete the Monday 'off-peak' services, and this took effect on 19th July 1965.

The running time from Orpington to Biggin Hill was 26 minutes, so the return trip was comfortably within an hour. The two-hourly frequency was operationally inefficient with paid staff, and the suggestion that it should be increased to hourly came from the volunteer drivers, who preferred to be active. An hourly frequency began on 1st September 1965 (The revised timetable actually began on 31st August, but there were no off-peak services on Mondays).

The doubling of the frequency placed further strain on the vehicles. The Austin required virtually no attention beyond routine servicing and tyre maintenance. The only replacement part it ever needed was a bottom hose when it arrived at Biggin Hill one morning in a cloud of steam. The Trojan, on the other hand, seemed to spend much of its time in the garage costing money rather than out on the road earning it. It reminded me of the little girl who had a little curl right in the middle of her forehead. When it was good, it was very very good, but when it was bad it was horrid.

It was decided to replace both of them with two new minibuses.

The most suitable vehicles available at the time were the Commer 12-seat 2500 series which were still entering service as postbuses nearly 20 years later, with a few modifications. The exchange was made in October 1965.

Being of light construction, the Commers were easy on fuel, returning about 35 m.p.g. on the bus route from the Perkins 4.99 diesel engines, but the gearboxes suffered too easily from lack of sensitivity on the part of the drivers. The passenger door mechanism included an automatic step, whose operating levers were easily bent when 'tucking in' to the bank in the narrow lanes, which was often necessary when meeting other vehicles. This was changed on the postbuses to an inbuilt step, which we would have much preferred.

FPM 283C setting-down at Orpington Station, Crofton Road.

The Harrington body conversion included a raised roof over the gangway to meet the headroom requirements for p.s.v. minibuses. The upper part of the raised section was a well for carrying luggage, accessed by folding steps on the main pillars, but this had no practical use on the bus service, and the vehicles were very little used for private hire. The makers were persuaded, with some difficulty, to extend the centre section forward to a peak in which was a roller-blind destination indicator. The sides of the raised roof section, and the rear doors, were used for commercial advertising, which provided valuable additional revenue.

At this point there was a brief essay into Sussex, where a London Transport route (852) had been withdrawn, and the local residents, the Rusper Parish Council and the Horsham Rural District Council were interested to know whether something on the same lines as the Orpington Rural Transport Association could be set up.

It was agreed that the Association would make a vehicle available for five Saturdays at a nominal mileage cost, and I would give my services, to test the response. The R.D.C. produced the publicity and the Parish Council distributed it, and the service ran from 30th October to 27th November 1965 under the banner of North Sussex Rural Transport.

The response was actually quite encouraging, but there did not appear to be anybody locally to organise it, other than myself, and I felt that the area lacked the potential for more than a minimal level of service. The experience was to prove valuable later, however.

At Orpington, having increased the frequency to hourly throughout the day, it became necessary to provide a relief driver for an hour while the duty driver had a meal break. A traffic census revealed that the 12.08 from Orpington usually ran empty throughout, and the 12.39 from Biggin Hill carried one passenger from Biggin Hill to Berrys Green. Apart from the imbalance of cost and revenue there was the psychological factor to be considered of the relief driver (Molly or Yvonne) turning out to drive for an hour for one short-rider. The answer was obvious, wasn't it? Cut it from the timetable. This is when we discovered the Viability Of The Empty Bus. Those services were deleted from 1st January 1966, after which traffic generally declined. On questioning the passengers it became clear that they had lost confidence in the service pattern because they knew that there was now a gap in an otherwise regular hourly frequency, and they said they could never remember when it was. It would have been tempting to point out that they could easily remember, because the missing service was the one they had never used.

This demonstrates that there is a positive cash value to all the other hours of maintaining an hourly frequency even if one of the hours is expensive or inconvenient to maintain, and earns little or no revenue directly.

The level of activity was now such that the organisation of part-time staff, including the loyal band of volunteer Saturday drivers, the maintenance of vehicles and all the other incidental tasks, made it appear desirable to have a full-time employee who could take responsibility for the day-to-day operation. Miss Joan Normington, ex Women's Royal Army Corps vehicle maintenance instructor, had joined the staff in 1965 with a view to taking this on, and from 1st January 1966 she became Operating Manager, while I became (honorary) Commercial Manager.

The ORTA services had now been going for two and a half years, and from dealing only with optional journeys were coming to be relied on for more serious travel commitments during the day as well as journeys to and from work. The only regressive move had been the withdrawal of the Monday off-peak services after what may have been too short a trial.

The Association had met its first objective of creating a link between Biggin Hill, Berrys Green, Downe and Orpington. The hourly frequency proved encouraging, and it was felt that the route should be extended into the Valley, which was being rapidly developed. The first urgent need was for children to be conveyed between their new homes and the primary school in the village, too short a trip for them to qualify for statutory provision, but there was a general feeling that they would be safer in a vehicle than walking, even when accompanied.

Unfortunately, the earliest development was in an area to which the only surfaced access was by Polesteeple Hill. Looking back, it is so obvious that most of the problems facing the developers themselves, the new settlers, and the Association in its attempts to meet their needs for public transport, arose from the ineptitude of the local authority in failing to ensure the provision of adequate access roads. From April 1965 the authority responsible was the London Borough of Bromley, but it inherited the disastrous situation from the Orpington U.D.C., which had been planning this development for a decade, and yet was apparently oblivious to the consequences of the inadequacy of its preparation.

An unadopted road, Sunningvale Avenue, connected the foot of Stock Hill with the foot of Polesteeple Hill. Had this been made up before any building work started in the Valley, it would have permitted better access to the first stage of development. Traffic could have used the slightly wider Stock Hill rather than the frighteningly inadequate Polesteeple Hill. That alone would have made all the difference to the developers, the residents, and the Association's fortunes.

Not daring to suggest any sort of a service via Polesteeple Hill, which was really the most urgent need, the Association decided to apply for a licence to serve the north end of the Valley, to which access was by Stock Hill.

It would be necessary for this to be a 'stage carriage' because the children would be paying separate fares. The Police objected to the application for a Road Service Licence on the grounds that the route was unsuitable for any form of public service operation. One Monday I went to the offices of the Metropolitan Traffic Area at Bromyard Avenue, Acton (on the route of the former 607 trolleybus whose schedule I had written-up in 1953), to attend the public hearing of the application and explain the Association's desire to provide the service. As a matter of interest, the Metropolitan was the only Traffic Area in which the Traffic Commissioner was allowed to sit without a Deputy. I wondered what to expect.

During the hearing I thought the result was a foregone conclusion in view of the Police objection. To my astonishment, the Traffic Commissioner, Mr Muir, dismissed the objection and granted the application, having spent the previous afternoon (Sunday) carrying out a route survey personally.

Thus encouraged, we began to plan a more comprehensive public service for the Valley.

Stock Hill led down to the north end of the Valley and then

another narrow lane led up into the New Addington estate, which had some light industry and frequent bus services to Croydon. An extension of the ORTA route to New Addington could therefore be expected to develop some traffic.

The first phase of new building was at the south end of the Valley, accessible only via Polesteeple Hill, beyond which two lanes, one narrower than the other, led to Tatsfield. There was a continuous tattered ribbon of earlier low density development along the lane via Ricketts Hill, which fortunately was the slightly less narrow lane. From Tatsfield there were bus services to Oxted (infrequently) and Warlingham, the latter continuing to Croydon, but these had nothing like the same potential as the New Addington ones. On the assurance that Sunningvale Avenue was going to be made up 'soon', we planned a route pattern using it.

The plan was for two routes from Biggin Hill, both descending Stock Hill, then one via the as yet undeveloped north end of the Valley to New Addington, and the other via Sunningvale Avenue and Ricketts Hill to Tatsfield. These routes would be operationally efficient, the round trip on each taking a comfortable half-hour. One bus could do each alternately, but connections with the hourly Orpington services would have been only in one direction.

The solution adopted, with trepidation, was to plan each route on an hourly frequency right through to Orpington, which meant using three vehicles altogether and providing a half-hourly frequency along the original route from Biggin Hill to Orpington. It was expected that traffic originating from both routes through the Valley would justify the increase in frequency, especially as development spread to the north end.

We now understood that Sunningvale Avenue would be completed within the current financial year, i.e. by the end of March 1967, so the new timetables were planned for introduction on 28th March, and in order to operate them two pre-used Commers were purchased. These had the converter's standard p.s.v. roof but no destination indicators, and one had a petrol engine. This was reserved as far as possible for the school contract which had been gained in Orpington, only being used on the bus route if one of the diesels needed urgent attention. Routine servicing of all the vehicles was done during the off-peak period on Mondays, when the bus service was not operating.

A pre-used Commer with the Harrington standard roof beside one with the specially-modified roof in the Council yard at Orpington.

To staff the services, there were four duties. One was covered by Miss Normington, two by young women whom she recruited from the W.R.A.C., and the fourth by the existing part-time and volunteer drivers.

As with so many local authority projects, serious slippage occurred in completing Sunningvale Avenue, so the Tatsfield route had to be diverted and missed the Valley altogether. The Association's resources were stretched by having to maintain the new pattern of services while being deprived of half of the anticipated extra revenue. The debilitating effect was so great that there was no option but to reduce the Tatsfield services. The reductions took effect gradually, because we lived in perpetual hope that the road would become available. Even when we eventually had to admit defeat and withdraw them altogether on 1st January 1968, the withdrawal was described as suspension rather than termination of service.

Feeling that we had been thoroughly misled by the Borough Council, an approach was made for financial support for the New Addington services in view of the benefits which they brought to the Valley.

The idea of local authorities grant-aiding public transport services was in the Transport Bill and would become Section 34 of the Transport Act 1968, taking effect on 1st January 1969, but was specifically for 'rural' services. The legislators carefully avoided defining 'rural'.

As with so much of its activity, in this the Association was ahead of its time, trying to achieve something by means which were unheard of then but have since become commonplace. However, the Borough Council did agree to make a loan of £500 to the Association on certain conditions, one of which was that there was to be no further expansion of activity until the loan was repaid. This was to be a contributory factor to the events which open the next chapter.

THE fact that a grant of £500 —not a free-of-interest loan of £2,000, is, apparently, not forthcoming from Bromley Borough Council, will cause great distress to many who rely on the Orpington Rural District bus service, which is used by young wives doing part-time work while their families are away, elderly and partially disabled persons, busy housewives, needing facilities not provided in the out-lying areas, and those attending medical, dental, welfare and chiropody clinics.

I have seen a copy of the statement of O.R.T.A.'s accounts (as already supplied to the local Council Treasurer) and note that the £2,000 you mention is probably the existing loan with Westminster Bank, upon which interest is being paid. Surely it is ludicrous to suggest that the needed £500 should be a further loan, with the additional expense of interest and repayment—especially as a grant of that amount would not even incur an increase of one farthing on the present rates!

The losses of O.R.T.A. are mainly due to cessation of a regular income from the Valley School bus service, and the failure of the Council to implement the promise of a through road to the Tatsfield area by last February, upon which promise the hire purchase of additional buses was undertaken to serve the new estates at that end of the valley. Incidentally, the purchase of these will be completed early next year, meaning very decreased loss, even if the through road has still not materialised.

I have heard many—even old age pensioners—state that they would prefer to pay increased fares rather than lose the service.

(Miss) C. M. SQUIRE
77, Sunningvale-avenue,
Biggin Hill.

[**Footnote**: As reported last week, Bromley Council's General Purposes Committee are offering a £500 *loan* instead of a grant. The £2,000 loan which he committee discussed and rejected was, it now seems, all a misunderstanding. See story on Page 2 this week.—Ed.]

Letter published in Kentish Times, 1968

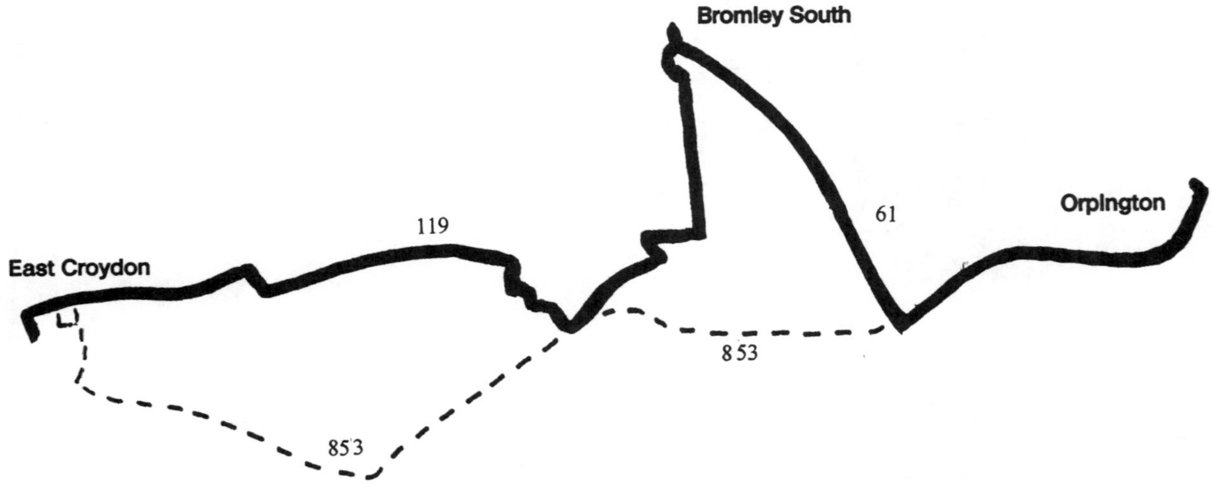

Routes 61 and 119 were the shortest way from Orpington to Croydon.

3. North Downs

For many years there had been another deficiency in the local public transport network west of Orpington. The direct distance from Orpington to Croydon is ten miles, but the journey by public transport used to be tortuous and time-consuming.

There were several ways of doing it, all about as good or bad as each other. However you went, the journey took about an hour and a quarter in theory. The cost was commensurate with the mode and convenience of the method chosen.

The easiest, most comfortable, most reliable and most expensive was by train via London. The route mileage was about 25, and the fare was charged accordingly. The trains from Orpington to Victoria ran every 20 minutes, and much more frequently from Victoria to Croydon. One easy change of train at Victoria was all that was required.

It was possible to reduce the mileage, and therefore the fare, by changing at Beckenham Junction and Crystal Palace, and also at Norwood Junction if it was important to arrive at East Croydon rather than West Croydon. Depending on how the connections worked, this was unlikely to be any quicker, and it was a lot more trouble.

As noted in chapter 3 of part 1, there was a bus route (54) from Beckenham to Croydon. A change of mode always carries a price penalty, and again it was probably no quicker overall.

The normally-accepted way of travelling from Orpington to Croydon by public transport was by bus, changing at Bromley between two different frequencies. There was a psychological element to this journey, in that having travelled from Orpington to Bromley on route 61, waited an indeterminate time for the route 119 bus, and then travelled about half the distance from Bromley to Croydon (by this time probably an hour or so after setting out), the observant traveller noticed a signpost reading 'Orpington – 4m'. There was thus an increasing demand for a more direct bus route.

In 1968 the ORTA partners took the view that it was unlikely that London Transport would grant consent for such a route, and even if they did, the Association could not contemplate operating it because of the resources required, and because the London Borough of Bromley had recently granted the Association a loan of £500 on certain conditions, one of which was that there must be no expansion of activity until the loan was repaid.

My wife Mary and I formed a partnership with Roy Edwards, mentioned earlier, to set up a separate organisation, and we adopted the name North Downs Rural Transport to signify a relationship with ORTA. We sought London Transport's consent to operate a route from Orpington War Memorial to East Croydon Station via Locks Bottom (Farnborough Hospital), Keston Mark, Coney Hall, Addington Village, Coombe Road and Park Hill.

Rather to everybody's surprise, consent was quickly given, subject to the usual sort of restrictions, namely a prohibition of local carriage between Orpington and Keston Park (to protect route 61 between Orpington and Lock's Bottom), and protective fares between East Croydon and those points on the route which touched L.T. routes, i.e. Coombe Road (64), Gravel Hill (130), and Coney Hall (119). It was also a requirement that the fare from Orpington to Croydon should protect the sum of the fares by routes 61 and 119.

We then applied for a Road Service Licence. After some time had elapsed, we enquired about the application, and the Metropolitan Traffic Area office explained that the delay was due to the objection by Orpington Rural Transport on the grounds of abstraction of traffic between Orpington and New Addington. The objection was of a 'holding' or delaying nature requesting the Traffic Commissioner to delay granting the licence until Easter 1969. Contrary to the requirements of the objection procedure, we had not received a copy from the objectors, and requests to both ORTA and the Traffic Area failed to produce a copy of it.

Enquiries of the ORTA partners revealed that the objection had been lodged by Miss Normington (manager) without reference to them. They said that they would not have authorised it if they had been asked, but they took no steps to have it withdrawn. The intention of amicability and co-operation between the two 'Rural Transport' undertakings was thus sadly frustrated.

Faced with 'marking time' until the following Easter, we purchased an Austin J2 petrol minibus which had previously been used to provide a replacement bus service over part of the route of the closed Somerset & Dorset railway. It was arranged differently from the ORTA J2, having mostly forward-facing seats but access only through the rear doors. It was not really suitable for bus work, therefore, but would do as a stand-by.

North Downs No 1.

Unfortunately, its Certificate of Fitness was on the point of expiry, and we made the mistake of putting the work of preparation for re-certification in the hands of the local Austin main dealers. There were certain modifications which had to be made to minibuses to meet the P.S.V. Construction & Use Regulations at that time, and the garage carefully removed these and replaced them with the manufacturer's standard parts. We cut our losses and traded it in for a new Ford Transit, fleet number 2.

I do not know what effect the Transit van had, but the passenger version completely transformed the minibus market. Apart from the still-inadequate headroom (4'11"), the 12-seat Transit diesel minibus was closer to the ideal for our purpose than anything previously on the market, except possibly the larger Commer, which was a little too large and too expensive for us.

The Transit was fitted with a Perkins 4.108 diesel engine which gave us 30 m.p.g. on the bus route and up to 40 m.p.g. on private hire work. The Ford seats were more comfortable than those found on many full-size buses.

In order to relieve the stark white finish, we originally intended to have a red waistband like the ORTA minibuses, but it was decided instead to have 10-inch bold red letters forming the fleet name NORTH DOWNS along the waist each side, and smaller (4") letters on the brow over the windscreen and across the rear doors below the windows. The ten-inch letters were larger than was usual on any p.s.v. at the time and attracted some attention. They would be considered very moderate now.

The people of Biggin Hill were used to the ORTA minibuses, but in general minibuses were very unusual vehicles on stage-carriage (local bus) services, so we did everything possible to make this small vehicle look like a bus. We fitted holders for a slip-board approximately 3' x 1' to be carried above the radiator grille, bearing the destination in bold lettering. Holders were also fitted to the roof sides so that three boards could be carried which, viewed as a whole, were reminiscent of the side-boards carried on the Green Line coaches. These read ORPINGTON CROYDON BUS SERVICE.

North Downs No 2, showing features mentioned in the text.
No 3 (petrol) and No 7 (another diesel) did not have the roof boards.

The boards had a tendency to rattle in the holders. This could be cured with small paper wedges, but if these fell out some drivers simply removed the boards.

Inside, across the front above the windscreen, was a bold NO SMOKING notice. The principle is common now, but in 1969 it was quite a bold move to prohibit smoking altogether. Normally, if separate smoking and non-smoking accommodation could not be provided it was assumed that smoking should be allowed. We thought it would be oppressive in so small a vehicle, and the maximum time any passenger would be in the vehicle was half an hour, so the prohibition was made from the start.

Acceptance of this rule was no difficulty in the case of the passengers, but it became quite a serious problem with some of the drivers, despite the fact that it is an offence for a public service vehicle driver to smoke while on duty. For some reason this is a regulation which has never been enforced, which makes it doubly difficult for employers to insist on its observance.

When I was working for L.T. Country Buses, the District Superintendent (South East) was Wally Henton. He told us he had been in Sevenoaks Bus Station one day, making a poor job of rolling a cigarette, when a driver said to him "Blimey, guv, I have to do mine with one hand".

One tip I picked up from Wally, which I have used at times, was to draw up his car at a bus queue and ask "Anybody going to .....? Somebody would always take the offer of a free lift, and he would spend the time getting them to tell him their opinion of the bus services.

Vehicles operating under Road Service Licences were required to carry copies of the time and fare tables. Timetables were always freely available on our buses, and the faretable was fixed centrally above the windscreen where the driver and passengers could easily read it. Tickets were printed at home on our small hand press in simplified Bell Punch style at first, but we soon found it hard to keep up with demand, so we hired some 6-unit Ultimate machines from Bell Punch.

As it had been necessary to dispose of the Austin J2, the question of a stand-by vehicle arose again. It was decided to take the plunge and buy a second new Transit. It was apparently impossible to have a diesel delivered before Easter, but we could have a petrol one immediately (has anything changed in 30 years?). This was otherwise identical to the first and became No. 3.

If another diesel had been obtainable, the two would have been fully interchangeable, but we intended to keep this petrol one strictly as a stand-by and for private hire, so the only 'bus item' fitted was the destination board holder.

While preparations were being made for the delayed introduction of the Orpington to Croydon route, it was learned that one of the Horsham operators, Mrs Mitchell (J & M A Mitchell) was intending to surrender her stage carriage licences. By chance, these were in the same area as the brief North Sussex Rural Transport experiment which had taken place more than three years previously. Despite the conclusion drawn then, which was of course based on the existence of the Mitchell services, a re-assessment of the potential which would follow withdrawal of those services led to the belief that the area would be suitable to conduct a more prolonged test of the viability of minibuses in a rural environment.

The Horsham Rural District Council was again interested in the proposal to maintain services in its District which would otherwise cease. The Clerk, Peter Soothill, was most helpful.

A traffic census of the Mitchell services was taken with Mrs Mitchell's permission, and the results discussed with Mr Soothill. There was a feeling that any reorganisation of services in the rural area north of Horsham should include access to the developing Crawley New Town, while recognising that the magnetism of the old-established market town of Horsham was still much stronger.

The Transport Act 1968 came into effect on 1st January 1969, only a week or two before the discussions with Mr Soothill took place. Under Section 34, County and County District councils were newly empowered to provide assistance by grant or loan to secure the provision, improvement or continuance of bus or ferry services for the benefit of persons residing in rural areas.

This was a new field for local authorities, so the R.D.C. sought advice from the Rural District Councils' Association, whose Assistant Secretary, Mr John S. Gilks, attended a meeting at Horsham to discuss the proposals. Mr Gilks' interest in transport matters may be better appreciated when it is known that he was a frequent contributor, especially of photographs, to the Railway Magazine, where his contributions were credited to J. Spencer Gilks. It was therefore a particular pleasure to me to meet him, and he continued to be a great help for many years subsequently.

The proposals discussed were that the irregular and infrequent services which were to be withdrawn should be replaced by a regular two-hourly frequency of minibuses, with an extension of one of the routes to Crawley. The weekly service to Pease Pottage carried so little traffic that it was impossible to propose its continuance.

At this point a fundamental error was made which probably altered the whole course of the history of 'North Downs', owing to our inexperience of local authority procedures. The O.R.T.Association was formed of councillors in their capacity as private citizens and had nothing to do with the Council as such, so experience of dealing with local authorities, which was needed now, had not been acquired.

In making it clear what the R.D.C. was now empowered to do, the Clerk was not giving any undertaking that it would exercise those powers, of course, but we interpreted it that the Council would assist if it was found that the new services were not self-sufficient, and this caused a considerable difficulty later.

Mrs Mitchell was surrendering her licences but not closing her business, so she still required her vehicles and premises. Her bus driver, Vernon Brock, elected to remain with the service under its new proprietors, so staffing was not an immediate problem.

It was not going to be possible to introduce minibuses immediately, so Mrs Mitchell agreed to let us use her coach during the transitional period. This was a 41-seat Bedford SB with a manual door which she had been using without a conductor, although it did not comply with the one-man operation rules.

We were anxious to 'play it by the book', so we arranged to employ a conductor when we became responsible for the operation. He would then become the second driver when we changed to minibuses. He did not turn up for work on the first day (8th April 1969) or subsequently, however, so Vernon simply carried on in his usual way.

The limits for one-man operation were 20 seats normally, but 32 seats if the door was directly under the driver's observation, so we quickly bought a Bedford C521 29-seat coach, TUX 416, which became our No 4.

The 29-seat coach, No 4, on a test run at the Croydon terminal.

In taking over the Road Service Licences from Mrs Mitchell, an application was made for revised time and faretables as an interim measure until the change to minibuses could be made, and dispensation was granted for these to be operated from the outset.

When the substantive application was published in Notices & Proceedings, it attracted an objection from Southdown Motor

Services Ltd (E.G.Dravers, Traffic Manager) on the grounds of abstraction. This was a patently absurd objection, so we enlisted the support of the Rural District Council and awaited the Public Sitting.

Three months elapsed and nothing further was heard about a sitting, so we made enquiries and were told that no sitting would be arranged unless agreement between the parties was clearly impossible, and it was up to the applicants to take the initiative in trying to come to an agreement with the objectors.

We pointed out that no specific ground of objection had been stated. The Traffic Area staff said they understood there was a question of fares, which they were expecting to be the subject of a modified application following discussions between the parties.

As we clearly did not understand the protocol, the Traffic Area staff took pity on us and elucidated the fact that Southdown's objection was based on the fear that our application, if granted, **might** entitle us to convey **children** between Horsham Carfax and Horsham Station for one **halfpenny** (old currency) less than their own authorised fare. The children's fare clause was clearly stated on the faretable which formed part of our application, including the words 'fractions of a penny charged as a penny', so the Traffic Area staff were able to negotiate withdrawal of the objection.

Once this was done, dispensation was given immediately for the revised services to be introduced.

The delay occasioned was several months, and the most disturbing features of the incident were: first that the objection should be submitted by an apparently responsible organisation with only a cursory glance at the application and without properly studying it, and worded so vaguely that its basis was unclear; secondly, that the basis, when elucidated, was so obviously spurious and unfounded; and thirdly, that it could be accepted by the Traffic Area without query.

The introduction of the Orpington to Croydon services, and the re-organisation of those in the Horsham area, had both been delayed by mischievous objections. In both cases this probably did us a favour, although the intention was malicious.

Our ignorance of the protocol when dealing with objections was obvious to the Traffic Area, and it would have been helpful to have had it explained to us earlier. It would have been better still if their practice had been to refuse to accept unfounded objections.

No 3 sandwiched between No 4 and the Brown Motor Services Nimbus, which later became North Downs No 16, at Horsham.

In the meantime, the Orpington to Croydon services were releasing the suppressed demand for a more direct route than previously available, and beginning to attract new traffic by stimulating latent demand.

The original 12-seat Transit, No 2, was used initially to provide services on Mondays to Saturdays which were timed at Croydon at 0845, 1045, 1245, 1445, 1645 & 1745. They normally left Orpington 30 minutes earlier, but on Mondays to Fridays the first service was given an extra 10 minutes to allow for traffic congestion on the approach to Croydon.

Orpington Rural Transport was a Community Bus Scheme, and I had been happy to act in an honorary capacity while teaching full-time. North Downs was a commercial organisation on a small scale which was expected to grow. The school where I taught was about to be closed as part of an education reorganisation scheme, so I took a part-time post at Lee in south-east London. I worked there on four mornings and Wednesday afternoon each week. We employed two part-time drivers: Peter Smith, for the first two services each morning, Mondays to Fridays, and Mrs Woodhead, always known as Woody, on Tuesday afternoons and for the midday service on Thursdays. My wife, Mary, covered the midday service on Mondays, Wednesdays and Fridays, and also the 1415 service on Wednesdays when I was at school. I drove the remainder of the services. This arrangement was very satisfactory. Peter and Woody were reliable, the wages bill was modest, and we went out to dinner when the week's takings reached £40 for the first time, in the second week of July.

Not long after we began operating our services, a young teenager with a freckled face and an infectious smile took to opening the door of the minibus at Keston Mark and asking if he could act as conductor. We were pleased at the interest he took and he was a great help to us in many ways throughout the years when North Downs was operating. He is mentioned again at the end of this chapter.

Travelling to work is a more serious business than going shopping, so it is only to be expected that commuter traffic is slower to build up. We were very gratified that there were two brave souls who used the commuter service on the first day, Tuesday 8th April 1969, and the number doubled during the week.

On our first anniversary, one of them, Mr Pope, wrote "Having seen the service grow from one bus carrying two passengers a year ago to the present vastly improved service, I wish North Downs every expansion for the future. Not only are they providing an essential service, but the punctuality and cheerfulness of all the staff are something which should be enjoyed by everyone".

Another passenger, H. Jordan, wrote "Like all the other passengers, I found the introduction of the service a Godsend. What I had not expected was the friendly atmosphere. Drivers and passengers seem to positively welcome the daily journeys. Long may the service continue to grow and prosper".

The growth of off-peak traffic could easily be accommodated by increasing the frequency to hourly through the day. The London Transport Central Bus standard average speed of 12 miles per hour would have resulted in a journey time of 51 minutes for the 10.2 miles, but we comfortably covered the distance in 27 minutes with the minibuses, except on the first journey on Mondays to Fridays. This was delayed by traffic congestion and the arrival time at Croydon varied by up to half an hour. We either got in front of the traffic and arrived early, or were delayed by it to arrive very late. It seemed to be impossible to arrive on time.

We began to think that we ought to identify our services by route numbers. We had a twinkle in our eye about providing Sunday services to the Ramsden estate in Orpington, currently provided by London Country Bus Services under the number 493, but this had been re-numbered from 854 when it was no longer necessary to use the 800-series numbers. We also proposed to cover the former 852 route from Horsham to Crawley when the planned service pattern came into full operation, so it seemed that it would be appropriate to use numbers up to 852 at Horsham and numbers upwards from 854 at Orpington. 853 had been used by London Transport in Crawley, so we thought it would be best for it to be allocated to our main route from Orpington to Croydon.

This development, and the prospect of revised timetables for both areas, encouraged us to produce better quality publicity in the form of properly printed leaflets. We went to Holmes the Printers in Horsham for a quotation. The proprietor (Freddie Shephard) looked at the copy and said "Ah, buses. Do you know, a young man from Christ's Hospital (school) came in here one day in the war asking me to print lists of railway engine numbers. He said to me 'I can't pay you for them, Sherlock, until I've sold them'. His name was Ian Allan". We felt that we were following in a good tradition, so we placed the order.

A new timetable providing for increased levels of service in both peak and off-peak periods on route 853 was introduced on 2nd September 1969. A second vehicle was required for the peak

853 INTERCHANGE DIAGRAM

EAST CROYDON STATION	Trains and buses to all parts of Surrey and Sussex (e.g. GATWICK AIRPORT BRIGHTON, etc.)
COOMBE ROAD STATION	Trains during Monday to Friday peak hours only.
ADDINGTON Gravel Hill	Bus 64 to Selsdon. Bus 130 to New Addington.
CONEY HALL	Bus 119 to West Wickham and Shirley. Bus 119 & 138 to Hayes and Bromley.
KESTON MARK	Bus 410 to Biggin Hill, Westerham, Oxted, Godstone, Redhill & Reigate.
LOCKS BOTTOM Farnborough Hospital	Green Line 704 to Sevenoaks, and Tunbridge Wells.
ORPINGTON STATION	Trains to all parts of Kent.
ORPINGTON MEMORIAL	Buses to all local areas.

LOCAL BUS and TRAIN TIMETABLES, 1/-, for Croydon and Bromley/Orpington areas, are available on North Downs buses, when published

periods (Mondays to Fridays), and for more than a month every vehicle we possessed was committed to scheduled requirements; we had no spare vehicle if anything went wrong.

The increase in commuter traffic thus meant having to obtain another bus. The Ford dealers who had supplied the two 12-seat Transits were Gilbert Rice Ltd of Horsham. They interested us in a new Special Vehicle Option being built by Strachans of Hamble (Hants) as a parcel van or personnel carrier on the Transit chassis. The particular attraction was the interior headroom of 6'1". The body was slightly wider than the basic Ford van used to convert to the 12-seat p.s.v. version, and could accommodate four rows of 2+2 seating, making 16 in all. A visit to Hamble was arranged.

We found that the passenger vehicle presented a very spartan appearance, inside and out, due partly to the very square framing and the unattractive seating, described as 'stage-carriage standard'. I never did understand why bus passengers were supposed to be content with hard seats.

No 5 at the first North Downs terminal stand at Orpington, for minibuses. The terminal working and stand were altered when larger vehicles were introduced.

The angularity of the body was softened at the front by a roof dome above a large curved windscreen, but the back was absolutely square-cut.

A North Downs 16-seat Transit on loan to Orpington Rural Transport at Downe heading towards New Addington. Note the very square-cut rear, which was thought to be very austere at the time. People became familiar with the appearance later, when London Transport and the National Bus Company introduced them in considerable numbers. The ORTA Commer facing the camera is actually going to Orpington, showing the wrong destination.

We suggested a few detail improvements to make the vehicle suitable for public service work. First, the approaching vehicle should be recognisable as a bus, and identifiable as the right bus, so a destination indicator should be incorporated; secondly, the door should be power-operated; thirdly, the seats should be more comfortable, and more visually welcoming. Those in the 12-seat vehicles, which were in-built by Ford and not part of the p.s.v. conversion, were excellent.

Strachans were somewhat taken aback, but agreed that the seats might be possible. The other items, they regretted, would not.

A further complication was that Ford had not approved a diesel version of the 35cwt parcel van because the additional weight of the diesel engine and the steel sliding doors of the body might overload the front axle in certain circumstances. They also feared that the vehicle might be underpowered because the diesel engine used in the Transit at the time (before the disastrous 'York' engine) was the Perkins 4.108 (1760cc) of 52 b.h.p., which compared with the 85.5 b.h.p. of the 2-litre petrol engine (as used in the Corsair car).

There were six rear-axle ratios available. Passenger vehicles needed to be fairly high-geared to achieve an adequate top speed while low top speeds were still thought to be acceptable for goods vehicles.

In order to obtain a vehicle as quickly as possible, it was decided to order one in its standard form which could be taken from stock. This meant a petrol engine, a mid-ratio rear axle, standard stage-carriage seats, manual door and no destination indicator. A kit for the latter was available, and Gilbert Rice Ltd constructed a box suspended from the crossbeam so that the display showed through the top of the windscreen, which was very satisfactory. This vehicle became No 5.

The high body naturally created more wind resistance than the smaller vehicles, and used at least 50% more petrol than No 3, so it was important to us to persuade Ford to make a diesel version available. They did so because a full load of passengers is a predictable weight, whereas goods vehicle loading varies considerably according to the density of the items carried.

For No 6 Strachans modified the roof dome to include a destination screen, and fitted Ford seats, so the only remaining difficulty was the door. The axle was slightly higher-geared than No 5 and made this one a better performer on the road than any that we had subsequently, which Ford insisted had to be lower-geared.

Having obtained dispensation from the Traffic Commissioner to revise the pattern of services, following the withdrawal of Southdown's objection, it was necessary to obtain another vehicle to operate them. The timetables were printed with a start date of 6th October 1969, but No 5 was not delivered until the 7th, so the start date had to be amended to 9th October.

The driver who had previously been employed by Mrs Mitchell, Vernon Brock, proved to be a thoroughly good-hearted, cheerful, enthusiastic young man. We were fortunate that he introduced us to another local driver, Gordon Harris, who had been working for A.T.Brady (Brown Motor Services) of Forest Green. Gordon had been a fireman on steam locomotives on the Horsham to Guildford line and turned to bus driving when the railway closed. His wife, Anne, also became the holder of a p.s.v. licence for minibuses, so there were three drivers available to cover the six weekdays. No services ran on Sundays.

Gordon, Anne and Vernon with the Horsham allocation 'on shed'.

The traffic pattern in the area was long-established, unlike that on the Orpington to Croydon route. Changes were seen as a disruption of people's habits rather than as fresh opportunities for travel. The intention of the change to a pattern which could be operated with minibuses was to widen choice. The new pattern of services at Ockley, for example, increased the opportunities for travel to Horsham, and created new opportunities to travel to Crawley. It was hoped that the peak of demand, previously at 10.35 a.m. on Fridays, would be spread into a more general demand pattern.

Instead of seizing the new opportunities presented by the minibuses, the residents of Ockley continued to travel at 11.00 a.m. on Fridays, filling the minibus and thus causing consternation at points further along the route, especially at Warnham. Loadings from Ockley were 0 or 1 at other times.

We were still struggling to adjust departure times from Orpington to achieve the desired punctual arrivals at Croydon, and there was such an adjustment on 15th December 1969. After that, however, the timetables in both areas remained unmolested for some time.

The 29-seat coach really had to be withdrawn on Christmas Eve 1969, when No 6 was delivered. It was our plan to have three minibuses operating the Horsham area network, but for the time being at least, we could only use two. Such was the pressure on the Orpington to Croydon route that we had to devise a way of meeting the Horsham needs with two 12-seaters until we could get some more sixteens.

We had been able to locate another diesel 12-seater in build at Manchester, and we had to have it at Horsham in time for the start of the school term on 7th January 1970. No 7 was driven overnight from Manchester and arrived at 0615, going into service an hour later.

There was no doubt that the two sixteens, 5 & 6, were needed in both areas, but we had to deploy the three twelves. The compromise reached was to have one of each at Horsham, and the remainder at Orpington, i.e. one sixteen and one diesel twelve, with the petrol twelve as a spare.

The next 16-seat vehicle, No 8, was supplied with very low gearing, so that it was uncomfortable and embarrassing to drive, with the engine screaming in top gear at speeds above 30 m.p.h. It was the first to have a power-operated door, however, which was driven by a windscreen-wiper motor pulling wires attached to the door. This was fine until the wires broke. The operating switch kept the motor running when the door was fully open or closed if the driver did not release it at precisely the right moment, and this placed extra strain on the wires, but we were grateful to Strachan's for making the effort.

The capacity situation improved with the arrival of No 8 in April. Standing passengers are not allowed on 12-seat minibuses, but the sixteens could carry five (one-third of the seating capacity). Their payload was thus 75% greater than the twelves.

Route 853 approached Croydon via Addington village, near which was a new development by Wates the builders called Forestdale, rather further than comfortable walking distance from the bus stop at the foot of Gravel Hill. The developers provided a free minibus service, the 'Forestdale Express', from the estate to the bus stop. They enquired whether we would like to provide a commercial service which they would help us set up.

The Forestdale Express.

We were told we could take over the vehicle and the driver. The Commer minibus (similar to the ORTA vehicles) was not really suitable for the sort of services we provided, but we did give Winston a job.

Wates loaned us £750 to put down as a deposit on another 16-seat minibus, and it was agreed that we would begin the services on Monday 24th August 1970.

We devised timetables to operate the Forestdale route (855) by jazzing it off route 853 at Croydon. This scheduling slang means that the buses would work from Orpington to Croydon, then go to Forestdale and back, then return to Orpington.

It was obvious that the traffic from Forestdale would be heavily graded - another scheduling term meaning that there would be a great difference between the level of demand in peak and off-peak periods. We hoped that we would be able to cope with the peak demand with the frequent services we planned (every 15 minutes), and that the off-peak traffic would be stimulated (latent demand again) by the regular half-hourly frequency during the midday period and on Saturdays.

No 8 at Forestdale, awaiting departure to Croydon. At the right of the picture are Peter Larking and Barry King.

Route 853 was doubled in frequency to the same level. Sunday services were every two hours, and included the services to the Ramsden Estate (route 854). Evening services scaled down and would be described by a scheduler as 'irreg', but they were not as irregular as the word suggests.

The peak vehicle requirement for these services was six. Six! - sixteen months after commencement of route 853 with one 12-seat minibus every two hours.

We took delivery of the next 16-seat Transit, No 9, on 8th July 1970, and it worked one trip from Horsham to Crawley. When it returned we consulted the lads at Gilbert Rice Ltd about the ticking sound, which we assumed to be something minor.

They all went white, and said "It's picking up". The expression was meaningless to me, but apparently it was a broken piston ring scoring the cylinder, so it had to go back for a new engine, and it was redelivered to us on 31st July.

After this false start, we appreciated two things about this bus. First, it was higher geared than No 8, though not as good as No 6, and the door operating mechanism was fitted with microswitches which cut off the power on full travel, thus lessening the strain on the wires and the motor. We felt that we had arrived at our ideal minibus.

The ten-inch lettering used on the sides of the earlier minibuses had attracted attention because it was larger than usual, bus fleet names generally being modestly displayed. We thought we were now well enough known to be able to avoid the charge of flamboyance, so the lettering on the sides of No 9 and subsequent vehicles was a more normal four inches.

When the Forestdale route began on Sunday 23rd August 1970, and the frequency of route 853 was dramatically increased, the p.v.r. was six at Orpington. With the two in use at Horsham, the total of eight was actually one more than we possessed. For two weeks we necessarily failed to operate the full scheduled peak frequency. No 10, identical to No 9, was delivered on 9th September, but still we needed one more as a spare.

The usual Ford syndrome operated - wait for a diesel or take a petrol one immediately. We had little option, so No 11 was another petrol guzzler with a body identical to Nos 9 & 10, and was delivered on 1st October 1970.

We were now apparently secure in our ability to meet our scheduled commitments, but this was the point when we discovered that Transits are built with car-quality components. The significance of this arises from the work-load imposed upon them.

The average annual mileage of National Bus Company buses at

this time was about 33,000. Our minibuses did 100,000. One of the reasons for this was the high average speed, which enabled a minibus to travel from Orpington to Croydon and back in only three minutes more than London Transport Central Buses would have allowed for the one-way trip. This accounts for half the difference. The remainder can only be the difference in the 'peak grading', the number of spare vehicles, and the schedule efficiency.

Peak grading on the Orpington routes was 100%, i.e. the frequency doubled in the peaks. At Horsham it was 0%; the two buses were fully occupied throughout the day with no additional vehicle required. The average peak grading on London Transport and National Bus Company services was nothing like our average of more than 50%.

London Transport used to reckon on having 10% spare vehicles, but the N.B.C. had a purge on idle capital, and I heard of one garage in Leicester with a scheduled output of 204 buses which had its spare allocation reduced to zero!

The clue to the apparent discrepancy was schedule efficiency. Our minibuses had very little spare time between services. We worked on the basis that a moving bus **might** earn some revenue, but a stationary bus certainly could not.

London Transport kept a tight hold of stand time in the Central Area, to the point of scheduling ridiculous frequencies in order to keep it down. The frequency of route 229 at one time was 19 - 19 - 19 - 20 - 19 - 19 - 20, solely because, once a precedent was set on stand time at the ends of a route, it could never subsequently be reduced. In the case of route 229, it ensured that passengers could never work out when the buses were due, so they didn't use them.

The N.B.C. companies were much more relaxed, and excessive wasteful layover between services is the only other factor which could account for their low average mileage per vehicle, apart from the inexorable decline in evening and Sunday services which has been going on since the fifties.

A 'heavy duty' bus was depreciated over twelve years and probably lasted much longer. When the N.B.C. eventually came round to the idea of using minibuses, many years after the period we are currently considering, they had no experience ('track-record') of using them, so they decided to depreciate them over five years, and were surprised when some of them lasted longer. Again, this was due in most instances to the fact that they were normally used to provide services around housing estates, with a very low average speed, plenty of layover between services, and no services at all in the evenings or on Sundays.

We found that our Transits needed the first round of replacement parts at about 75,000 miles, i.e. about nine months from new. Two lasted for nearly three years, but in the latter part of that time they were mostly kept on light duties.

No 8 at Keston Park (east of Keston Mark). This was the last picking-up point towards Orpington, to 'protect' route 61. For many months after these Bus Stop signs were erected at North Downs stops the technical press were publishing claims by other operators to be the first to use the new standard designs. Now you know who really was. The design of the bus on the sign was changed PDQ because of representaions from the industry that the original was too old-fashioned. It is strongly reminiscent of a Bristol SC.

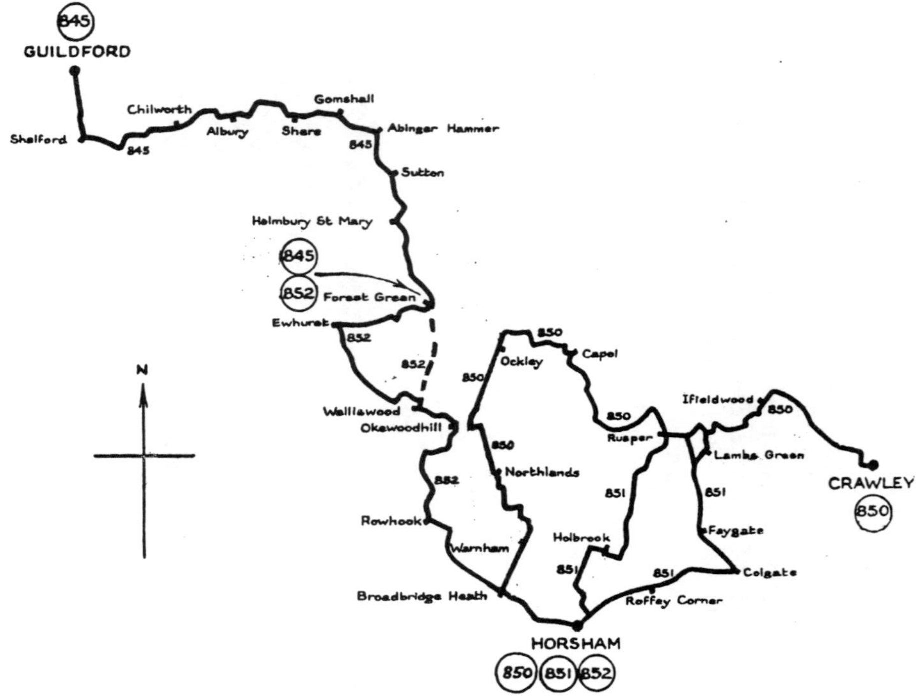

The North Downs Horsham area showing the integration of the Brown Motor Services routes with the developed Mitchell network after November 1970.

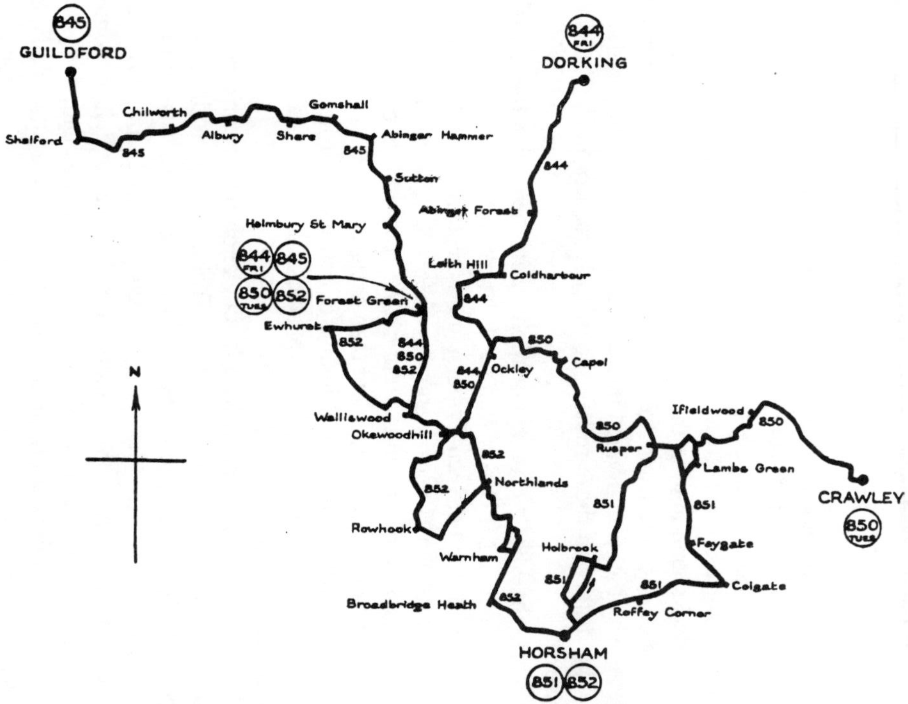

The North Downs Horsham area routes, February 1972.

There were two independent operators in the Horsham area. We took over the services of J. & M. A. Mitchell when Mrs Mitchell surrendered her licences in April 1969. The other was A. T. Brady of Forest Green, trading as Brown Motor Services. He had a route for many years from Forest Green to Guildford, occupying one bus and two drivers.

Kilner's had operated services in the area until 21st December 1954, when Southdown and London Transport obtained Unforeseen licences to continue them. One was a local service between Horsham and Roffey Corner via Littlehaven, operated by double-decks, and among the others were the country routes from Ewhurst to Horsham and from Horsham to Crawley via Lamb's Green, which L.T. combined into one through route numbered 852. For the history of these routes see Alan Lambert's book 'Hants & Sussex'.

When the substantive applications were heard by the Traffic Commissioners, Mr Brady won the Ewhurst to Horsham route, and added the section between Ewhurst and Forest Green. L.T. retained the route between Horsham and Crawley, but withdrew it in 1965, as mentioned in the previous chapter. We revived it in our October 1969 timetable, more by accident than design.

In 1970, Mr Brady was thinking of retiring, and invited us to purchase his house, garage and business. The transaction was completed on 2nd November 1970.

The question of premises had been exercising us considerably. When we took over the Mitchell services and bought the 29-seat coach, Vernon was able to park it overnight near his house in Broadbridge Heath. Similarly, when the first minibus was introduced in October 1969, Gordon and Anne kept it at home. Servicing was carried out by Gilbert Rice Ltd at Horsham.

The first minibus at Orpington was parked beside my mother's house, in a very useful side-road where we could see it from our flat opposite. This road alongside my mother's garden led to a few houses but was quite wide and three minibuses could be parked on it out of everybody's way.

An environmental inspector came to investigate a complaint

from one of our neighbours, took one look at the situation, laughed heartily, and wrote back telling them not to be so silly.

By the time the Forestdale route was added, and the number of minibuses was seriously increasing, the vehicles went home with the drivers. They could do that quite legally in those days; it wouldn't be allowed now. We were then fortunate to be offered the tail-end lease on a building suitable as office and garage, with a yard, which had been Morphy-Richards' original factory. Its earlier provenance was revealed by its address - Oasthouse Way. We thus had parking and servicing facilities in both of our operating areas.

The vehicles acquired with the Forest Green business we numbered as follows, omitting 13 because some of the staff were superstitious:

12 1950 Leyland Comet 32-seat Duple;
14 1961 Bedford SB 41-seat Harrington Crusader;
15 1963 Bedford VAS 29-seat Marshall Cambrette;
16 1959 Albion Nimbus 31-seat Willowbrook.

The three buses had driver-controlled doors, not powered, but operated with mechanical linkage from a large lever in the cab.

The Comet was a really solid vehicle. Rumour had it that a dent on the nearside had been caused by a car ramming it full-tilt from a side road, but it was not clear whether the car had been a Rover or a Jaguar. There was general agreement that if it had hit the Bedford it would have gone right through and out the other side.

The Comet, No 12, at Forest Green, with a corner of an unrepainted Western Welsh Nimbus just visible behind.

Mr Brady had bought the Comet new in 1950, and assured us that it was sound mechanically. He said "The old lady's been six times round the clock, or seven, I can't remember which, but she's all right because she had new piston rings ten years ago". The king pins were tapered, and adjustment for the annual inspection took a few minutes. Over the years we have spent a great deal of money replacing the king-pins on other vehicles. The local agents could usually supply spare parts off the shelf, or they came the next day.

The Comet was flat out with every rivet rattling at 38 m.p.h., and at 28 the driver **had** to know what was happening several hundred yards ahead if he was to have any chance of stopping if something unexpected happened. You certainly didn't follow closely behind the vehicle in front. Many years later I was told it should have had a servo, but Mr Brady never mentioned it, nor did his mechanic or drivers. They were all used to it just as it was.

The Comet in action. Passengers boarding at Walliswood. My pet hate is photographers who wait for everybody to go away before they take pictures of a deserted bus.

Unfortunately, the Certificate of Fitness expired in April 1971. We kept it for a year and employed a young man to work on it for re-certification, but we lacked the funds and expertise to do it properly and it was eventually sold. I am glad to know it was preserved and last heard of it in Sheffield in 1993.

The coach was kept for school contract and private hire work and rarely, if ever, used on bus service.

The coach, No 14,
Bedford SB 41-seat
Harrington Crusader body

Zebedee No 15,
Bedford VAS 29-seat
Marshall Cambrette body.

The Bedford bus was a poor thing. Its appearance was not prepossessing; the door was in the position which was still normal for coaches at the time, behind the front wheels, so that the driver had to carry out his conducting duties over his left shoulder; the rear axle sounded very tram-like and could be heard approaching for the evening run-in practically all the way down the hill from Holmbury St Mary; and the suspension was so lively that one of the drivers nick-named it Zebedee. Nevertheless, Bert and Charlie used it on the Guildford route (845) without any trouble.

The Nimbus was the ideal mid-size bus. It was neat in appearance, manoeuvrable, comfortable to drive apart from being governed down too much, but this made it very economical, and bright and airy for the passengers. I often thought I should like a whole fleet of them. Alas, its CoF expired three months after the Comet's, and we had to part with it.

The acquisition of Brown Motor Services eased our vehicle availability situation a little, and the petrol 12-seat Transit, No 3, was withdrawn on Christmas Eve.

Faced with the need to replace the Comet and the Nimbus in April and July 1971, we bought three ex-Western Welsh Nimbuses with Weymann 30-seat bodies in March. They were sprightlier than the BMS Nimbus, whose four-speed gearbox combined with the governed-down pump made it rather sedate.

No 17, a Western Welsh Nimbus in the Brown Motor Services' chocolate and cream colours which were perpetuated on the North Downs vehicles based at Forest Green.

These Nimbuses had air-operated hinged doors about which the less said the better, and six-speed 'crash' boxes. I learned how to drive them one morning when I took one on our school contract picking up children all over Leith Hill and taking them into Dorking.

The roads on Leith Hill were like those at Biggin Hill - steep and narrow lanes, but at least there was not much traffic on them.

As I was making myself comfortable in the driving seat, our mechanic Roy Burstow gave me his usual cheery grin and said "By the way Sir (he always called me Sir), we have a little trouble with the clutch on this one today, so don't use the clutch to change gear, will you, Sir, or you'll very soon find you haven't got a clutch. Just use it for starting from rest". After that I hardly ever used the clutch to change gear on those Nimbuses. Clutchless changes were so easy with no synchromesh to keep fighting you. I remember an old East Surrey driver saying that clutches (for changing gear) were for poor drivers. What would he think of today's gear-changing arrangements?

On Sundays, the Forestdale services were so poorly used that from 23rd May 1971 they were withdrawn and the time utilised to provide services to the Roundshaw estate in Croydon, served on weekdays by route 233. This route was well-known to vehicle enthusiasts because it was the usual home of the front-entrance rear-engine Routemaster. What a pity politics prevented the building of a fleet of them; London Transport might have been saved such a lot of trouble with Atlanteans and Fleetlines.

The review of the Forestdale services revealed their weaknesses. The peak demand was too great, and the reliability was too haphazard, with delays caused by the traffic congestion in Croydon, despite our comparatively uncongested route. Our vehicle resources were always at full stretch, also.

The Orpington Rural Transport Association had been unable to take part in the creation of the new link to Croydon, which led to the formation of the North Downs partnership. Their manager took unauthorised action which removed the possibility of the co-operation which we had envisaged. They had replaced the Commers with 16-seat Transits which unfortunately had Ford's new 'York' diesel engine, which caused them enormous reliability problems.

Our Orpington foreman, John Maddison, left us and joined forces with the ORTA manager to form Orpington and District Omnibuses. They took over the Forestdale route on 21st June 1971 and operated double-deck vehicles, which would certainly have coped with the peak loads, but I doubt whether the reliability at Forestdale was any better.

Our operational capability was now improved, and so was our reliability. We were able to withdraw the two remaining 12-seaters, which had become something of an embarrassment on capacity grounds, causing waiting passengers to groan audibly when they saw one approaching. We also withdrew the first petrol sixteen, No 5, which was very heavy on fuel. These vehicles had all played a very important part in our development, but it was now time to move on.

It was with great regret that we withdrew No 6. With greater engineering resources of our own, we might have transferred the running gear to No 11, but the cost of having it done would have been prohibitive.

No 6 was the last of the hand-door stock. When we were running both manual and automatic sliding doors we found that passengers would often try to open the power doors manually, which again caused trouble with the wires. Similarly, on arrival at a stop with a manual door vehicle, the driver and passengers might spend a few seconds smiling at each other through the door window before the passengers realised that they had to open it themselves. We overcame that difficulty by putting small notices on the doors:-

AUTOMATIC DOOR - STAND CLEAR

and D - I - Y DOOR – SLIDE ⟹

One of our main problems was the cheap fares policy of the Greater London Council. I certainly have no objection to the policy in principle, but it was very unfortunate for us that it was in force just when we were trying to establish route 853.

It was a condition of London Transport's consent for the operation of the route that we should not undercut their fares, but equally we could not charge more without losing some passengers. While L.T. was compensated for holding its fares down, we were not, and so we were deprived of much-needed income.

One of the Western Welsh Nimbuses, No 18, had to be withdrawn after only five months, in August 1971, so for a time we hired a GS from Tillingbourne Valley. We took the opportunity to try it on routes 853/4/6 one Sunday and found it very satisfactory. We also tried a Nimbus, but decided that the strain of the suburban environment might be too much for it. This was reinforced by the fact that it broke down in service and had to be towed back to Forest Green by Tony McCann, who had the commercial garage next door.

The Albion Nimbus was not regarded very highly by the large operators, who found the constructional quality less satisfactory than that of the heavy duty vehicles which formed the bulk of their fleets.

The GS which we hired from Tillingbourne demonstrated the difference. London Transport thought of GSs as lightwieght, but we found that to be a strictly comparative judgement, because it was in a different league from anything in our own fleet.

Tillingbourne Valley had been operating GSs for some years on their routes from Guildford to Ewhurst and Guildford to Farley Green. The company had recently been bought from the Trice family by Trevor Brown, who dropped the word Valley from the title and set out to develop it. He persuaded us that the best buy on the second-hand market currently was the Bristol LS, which had been the standard single deck for the Tilling Group companies in the fifties.

There was a myth that LS stood for Light Saloon, but again this was a strictly comparative term. Our first one, No 20, arrived at Forest Green on 5th September 1971. Roy, our mechanic, looked at it apprehensively, and when he lifted the hatches and saw what he was going to be dealing with, his hair stood on end. He quickly recovered his composure and said "Well, Sir, we'll have a go". This was our first full-size heavy duty single deck bus.

The big companies sold vehicles about a year before the Certificate of Fitness expired. The purchasers could then decide whether to recertify them or simply run the CoF out and scrap them.

As mentioned in connection with the Comet, we lacked the funds and the expertise to put vehicles up for recertification, so we ran them until the CoF expired and then traded them in. Paul Sykes bought them in quantity from the big companies, re-sold the better ones and scrapped the rest.

Numbers 21 and 22 came to us from Western National in November 1971, having been Training Units - mobile classrooms used for training staff in preparation for decimalisation in February that year. Decimalisation was a big non-event, and Western National must have regretted setting-up a costly training programme which proved to be so unnecessary.

The worst effect of the change to decimal currency was inflationary. Suppliers very rapidly took advantage of consumers' perception that, while two shillings had been clearly two units, tenpence was only one.

The benefit to us of having these training units was that they had longer 'tickets' than the usual withdrawals, and needed only one set of seats to re-convert both of them to service buses.

The two Western National LS training units before repainting. No 21 is nearest the camera, 16-seat Transit No 10 behind, and No 22 in the distance.

The six-speed gearboxes on the Western Welsh Nimbuses might have been a sheer delight to use, but the four speed plus overdrive boxes on the LSs were not so easy.

The Gardner five cylinder engines were very slow revving, producing maximum torque at only 1800 r.p.m., and they were governed to 2200 r.p.m. The gearboxes had to be used, and they were (theoretically) synchromesh, which seemed to make them more difficult. The overdrive was incredible, access to it being direct from fourth, not from neutral. This meant that if you were going along in overdrive, minding your own business, when a situation developed requiring rather rapid deceleration, it was all too easy to miss the chance of dropping back into fourth. The only thing I could do when this happened to me was to come to a dead stand, exit overdrive through fourth into neutral, then go into first for a fresh start, with unspoken apologies all round to people who wondered what on earth was going on. I was very careful to avoid use of the overdrive in normal bus service after that.

Another acquisition in November 1971 (25th) was a Bedford OB, which we used on the Leith Hill contract.

Early in 1972 it became clear that the Horsham area services needed drastic action. Routes 845 and 851 were self-sufficient. Route 844, which ran on Fridays from Forest Green to Dorking, utilised a school contract vehicle and was very well used. The core of this route was the former L.T. route 433 between Coldharbour and Dorking, but we picked up a lot of people before we reached Coldharbour.

We decided that the other routes could only be operated on the same basis of providing public services in between school contract commitments, and we applied for changes accordingly.

The 1968 Transport Act had now been on the statute book for three years. The provisions of Section 34 were noted earlier, but the route which could have most benefitted from help (852) ran cross-border between Surrey and West Sussex, and neither Council wanted to do anything which could possibly be of advantage to the other. It was too late. We were in a downward spiral and suffering a great deal of lost mileage through non-availability of vehicles, routes 845 and 852 being the worst affected because they had no direct commitment to the conveyance of schoolchildren. On strictly commercial grounds, we would certainly not have chosen to cut mileage from route 845.

Minimal services had been maintained in the Horsham area until Tillingbourne took on routes 845 and 851 on 17th April 1972, while Tony McCann continued (or revived) route 852 in much reduced form, using the Bedford OB.

Enthusiasts who keep meticulous records of vehicle sightings will know that I have said nothing about other vehicles which were hired, such as the Bristol SC, which was more fun for the driver than the passengers. Inclusion of much detail in that respect, even if I had full and accurate records, would convert this from a reading book to a work of reference for a dedicated few, and those details are certain to be available from other sources for anyone who thinks they are important.

I think we would have managed better in the early seventies if the present system of a Certificate of Initial Fitness and an annual test had been in operation, so that we would not have needed to keep withdrawing vehicles as their Certificates of Fitness expired. The present annual tests are to a deadline and objective standards, whereas those we experienced were fairly haphazard, arranged as and when the vehicle examiners could fit them in. For most of our time the examiners were really pleasant and helpful, but for a short time we had one who wanted to intimidate us. Roy came into the office one morning in a hurry. "Sir, Sir, I see Mr **** coming up the drive, Sir. Have I your permission to bury him in the pit?"

We had already decided to transfer the remaining two LSs (21 & 22) to Orpington for route 853, which had a new timetable from 30th May 1972, increasing the running time to 35 minutes and reducing the off-peak frequency to hourly. The Sunday services on routes 853, 854 and 856 were withdrawn, the last day being the Bank Holiday Monday 29th May. The timetable required three vehicles for the peak periods, so two sixteens, 10 & 11, were retained to work with the LSs.

We were now diminished to being wholly dependent on route 853. The two LSs and two sixteens should have been adequate stock to meet the scheduled peak vehicle requirement of three, but we had trouble in the winter, so that a temporary timetable reducing the p.v.r. to two was operated from 15th January to the beginning of March 1973.

No 21 after repainting in the colours adopted at Orpington - blue and white separated by an orange band at the waist, with a logo that could be reproduced on a typewriter.

Another LS was purchased in mid-February, ex-United 2222 (222 CHN), which became our No 23. Somebody told me later that he knew that bus - it had spent the whole of its life on the Whitley Bay town service and had never been up a hill since it was made. Going up Crofton Pound hill first thing every morning must have been a shock for it, though that is only a pimple compared with some in United's territory.

Our foreman-driver-mechanic at Orpington was Colin Wiggins, who somehow managed to keep these vehicles going with not much to help him except his wits. The lease on Oasthouse Way had expired in 1972, and there was an uncomfortable gap before we obtained a similar tail-end lease on Old Fordyce Yard, also in St Mary Cray. During this gap, one at least of the buses was parked overnight on the terminal stand just round the corner from Colin's house. One morning he found that a section had been cut out of the control cable. It didn't defeat him, but it did delay the service for a while.

Colin had a nasty experience when he was working for London Transport, before he joined us. One Saturday night he was driving an RT on route 146 to Downe when a mini with three young people in it came walloping into the front of his bus at high speed and killed one of them. He said there was nothing he could do except pick up his feet and let them go underneath. It was a good job he had an RT, with its front engine, to give him some protection. That had not defeated him, either, and when he took a bus over from me one day, he joked as he adjusted the seat "I must have this seat further back; my doctor has told me to keep away from driving".

He paid me a back-handed compliment on one occasion when he said "Your trouble is that you always expect people to act intelligently". I find that you get the best people, and the best out of people, if you do that, and the others seem to disappear of their own accord.

There was one of the others who had to go, though I cannot remember now whether he jumped or had to be pushed. The first service to Croydon always took longer than the later ones because of the traffic congestion, and the timetable allowed for that. This driver took it upon himself to assume that the expanded running time should apply throughout, and re-wrote the whole of his duty accordingly, so before long he was scratching along only just in front of the following service, and stopped for his meal break just at the moment when he should have been starting again. He didn't come the next day.

The next vehicle arrival was quite different from the LSs. It was an ex-Green Line RF, and our drivers, who all had London Transport experience, fell upon it with glee. I was more impressed with its fuel consumption of only eight miles per gallon, compared with the incredibly economical LSs' 14 m.p.g. It arrived on the day No 21's CoF expired, 30th April 1973.

A month later, 29th May, another LS, No 25, arrived and two days later the petrol sixteen, No 11, was withdrawn. This vehicle, with about 40% of the seating capacity of an LS, used more fuel, but it was a bit quicker. We now had numbers 10, 22, 23, 24, and 25, plenty to ensure reliable operation, but the timetable was not as economic as it should have been, and we had to start planning one which would reduce the peak vehicle requirement to two.

The trouble was that the minibuses had been successful in attracting traffic in excess of their ability to cope with it economically at peak times. The larger buses were slower by about a minute a mile, and needed more terminal-working time. We could only provide an hourly off-peak frequency with two of them, compared with half-hourly with two minibuses. The traffic diminished to the point where it could have been handled adequately with 16-seaters again. We were in a dilemma. We had to reduce the resources required to handle the current level of peak traffic, but a reduction in peak frequency would result in a further reduction of traffic. We had seen what a stimulant frequency was, and we were now experiencing the reverse effect.

The timetable introduced on 27th October 1973 was the best compromise we could offer, but it relied more than we wished on the willingness of our passengers to concentrate their demand onto the services we could run. It was, in fact, almost the opposite of what we had been trying to achieve at Ockley four years earlier, and was little more successful.

When the Forestdale services were running, jazzed off route 853, the peak frequency on both routes was theoretically every 15 minutes. Later, the peak frequency with minibuses on route 853 alone was every 20 minutes. The first 'big-bus' timetable reduced the peak frequency to every 30 minutes using three vehicles. With only two buses, the peak frequency was reduced to specific timings, in order to maintain as far as possible the times which experience showed were the most in demand. This timetable was actually fairly suuccessful and was only changed the following year through another force of circumstance.

When it came into operation, the last 16-seat Transit, No 10, was withdrawn, replaced by yet another LS, No 26. To meet our p.v.r. of two, we had the RF and four LSs. In May 1974 I had the dubious distinction of driving the RF on its last journey in service.

During our first year of operation we had launched a news-letter called North Downs News, as a way of telling people in a chatty way what was going on in the firm, mentioning the drivers by name and so on. We could explain the operational difficulties, such as the effect of traffic congestion on reliability, and we found this was well received. It was produced on an 'as and when' basis, when we had something to say rather than because the calendar said it was time for one. Roy Edwards was Editor in chief.

One person who must be mentioned here, because he was very essential to the plot, is Trevor Adams. His business is insurance, but he is interested in buses. I wish we had known him earlier. We did not have a great number of insurance problems, but Trevor certainly helped us over those that we did have. He was also very useful in many other practical ways, but chiefly by simply being a friend at a difficult time. He now has an Interest with a capital I in several preserved buses.

The number of LSs gradually diminished as their Certificates expired and we acquired two MWs. They had six-cylinder engines, so were a little livelier. The MW type was similar to the LS, but bodied on a chassis, whereas the LS was of integral construction.

A further reminder of the purpose of buses. Passengers boarding an MW at Orpington Memorial, Spur Road stop, before departure for Croydon.

The circumstance which forced the next change was in 1974 when the lease on Old Fordyce Yard was terminated. It had been an open-ended tail-end lease 'until required for re-development', which we hoped would not be too quickly. In the event, we had very little time to find an alternative. We therefore decided to turn the wheel full circle and go back to 12-seat Transits, to reduce the journey time and build up the frequency again.

There seem to be few photographs of the last phase of North Downs minibuses. This one is from a colour print, and shows Stan Welsh about to depart to Croydon.

Servicing had been done by the very helpful Coney Hall Garage, who now offered us overnight standing space for one minibus. One was kept in the same side road which we had used previously, and the other went home with one of the drivers.

In 1975 we undertook responsibility for the operation of the Orpington Rural Transport route. Their 16-seat vehicles were necessarily withdrawn, and we hoped we could now realise our ambition to integrate the two enterprises. We gave their route the number 858, and planned some small developments which we hoped would improve the viability of the combined operation.

It was the change back to minibuses on route 853, which had been forced upon us rather than chosen as a strategy, which enabled us to do this, but again we found ourselves in a downward spiral which we could not reverse. In January 1976 Orpington and District took over the operation of route 853 and combined it with their Forestdale services as route 857. They experienced similar difficulties, however, and in due course they succumbed too.

Fortunately, there were two young men, Peter Larking and Gary Wood, who had always taken a keen interest in North Downs, and who now seized the opportunity to persuade Tillingbourne to help them set up a company which eventually became Metrobus Ltd. Peter was the teenager mentioned earlier in this chapter who used to act as conductor on our first 12-seat Transit.

We were gratified when they told us many years later that everybody was very sorry when North Downs ceased operation. To return the compliment, I can say that it gives me immense pleasure now to see how Metrobus has built on the enterprise we started.

My final word of thanks in this episode - last but certainly not least - is to my wife, Mary, who gave me unstinting support throughout this and subsequent activities, and our North Downs partner, Roy Edwards, who somehow kept track of transactions, which enabled accounts to be produced. It was my great good fortune to experience willing co-operation from so many other people also, that the efforts of the few who tried to 'put a spoke in the wheel' were largely frustrated. In the end, of course, Government agencies and financial institutions are no respecters of motives, intentions or efforts, only of results.

PART 3.

1. The Berwick area.

Berwick-upon-Tweed is the most northerly town in England. The town, as now recognised, consists principally of Berwick, Tweedmouth and Spittal. Berwick is all that part of England lying north of the River Tweed, Tweedmouth is on the south side of the river, and Spittal faces onto the sea south of Tweedmouth.

Berwick changed hands between the English and the Scots thirteen or fourteen times, depending on how you define the starting point. It was then still unclear whether it was in either, so it was quoted separately as a constituent of the United Kingdom, for example in the declaration of war with Russia in the mid-nineteenth century. During those hostilities, an Act was passed incorporating Berwick definitely into England, thus making it unnecessary to name it separately subsequently. This led to the myth that Berwick is still at war with Russia, which, during the cold war, induced a spine-chilling sense of occasion in American visitors.

Market day in Berwick-upon-Tweed, looking towards the Town Hall from the Scotsgate arch, with a taxibus approaching.

The village of Scremerston, about three miles south of the town, was within the pre-1974 Borough. Only half that distance, but just outside the old Borough, is East Ord. These villages have rural levels of bus service frequency.

The A1 (Great North) road and the East Coast main railway line pass through Berwick, which is approximately equidistant from Edinburgh and Newcastle upon Tyne. The nearest towns of similar characteristics to Berwick, other than strategic importance, are 25-30 miles away, at Dunbar (north), Kelso (south of west), and Alnwick (south).

Within Berwick's approximate 15-mile radius catchment area there are sundry small villages, those on the Scottish side being generally more substantial than the English ones. Eight miles up river, on the English bank, Norham has an echo of self-sufficiency, but is now more of a dormitory for Berwick businessmen. Nine miles north is the fishing port of Eyemouth, developing as a tourist attraction aided by European grants, with a population now above 3000.

Splitting the distance - and the magnetism - between Berwick and Alnwick is Belford, which probably never had much more going for it than that it was a staging point on the Great North Road. On the coast, about 25 miles south of Berwick, is the little fishing port of Seahouses. Offshore are the Farne Islands, at the outer end of which is the Longstone lighthouse. This was the scene of the epic rescue of the survivors from the unseaworthy 'Forfarshire' by Grace Darling in 1838. The Grace Darling museum is in Bamburgh, a village two or three miles north of Seahouses, which is overshadowed by its massive castle.

Bamburgh castle was well established by 604 A.D. (not in its present form, of course). North of Bamburgh is Holy Island (Lindisfarne), which alternates between being an island and a peninsula as the tide rises and falls. Transport to and from the island, after the horse and cart era, was by a fleet of Ford model T cars with specially raised suspension, which plied as taxis across the sands to and from Beal station until the causeway was built in 1956.

The causeway builders could not understand why the tides at night were so much more destructive than those during the day. Of course the causeway was going to kill the taxi business; but then, the islanders used to pray for ships to be wrecked on their shore so that they could plunder them.

About fifteen years later, a twice-weekly bus service began on Berwick market days (Wednesdays and Saturdays), which has the distinction of being one of very few to operate to a tide table.

Inland, Telford's direct road from Newcastle to Edinburgh passes through Wooler and Coldstream. These are of similar size, around 2000, making them small towns in this area. Their dependence on public transport is characterised by the fact that Wooler's railway passenger services were withdrawn in 1932. In the seventies, a survey of users of the Sunday evening bus to Newcastle revealed that it had been used from Coldstream by 12 passengers - in the whole of the summer! Possibly this was one actual passenger travelling each week except for holidays. The two towns are very approximately equidistant from each other and from Berwick, at more or less than 15 miles. Coldstream splits the distance between Berwick and Kelso.

A similar distance from Berwick, on the road going north of west, is Duns. The name derives from dune, meaning hill, and was the birthplace of the medieval scholar John Duns Scotus. He was discredited by Cromwell, which gave rise to the epithet dunce. The town's importance was increased by its status as County Town of Berwickshire from 1903 to 1975. People who do not understand the history are often puzzled by the fact that, while Berwick is now definitely in England, its shire has always been firmly in Scotland.

The population of Northumberland and the Borders is very sparse, but the distances to the major centres are so great that the towns have facilities and an importance out of proportion to their size. The traffic density is similarly thin, and we have our own glossary of terms here. Traffic congestion means I can see another car. **Severe** traffic congestion means it has had to slow down for some sheep. It is different on the A1, of course. Sometimes you can see three or four other cars and a lorry.

As you see, the A1 road at the Anglo-Scottish border is so busy that since these photographs were taken it has been made into a dual carriageway at this point.

2. Deregulation.

The Transport Act, 1985, contained provisions to de-regulate bus services. There was naturally a great deal of opposition to the Act on the part of those with a vested interest in maintaining their positions established in fifty-five years of the road service licencing system, as well as from politically motivated bodies and individuals.

The reluctance with which the licencing authorities relaxed their control of bus service provision was exemplified by the heading on Local Bus Service Registration forms. Operators now had an absolute right to register any service subject to the few basic rules, and the Traffic Commissioners could not refuse an application except on safety grounds, or unless it was improperly made. Refusal, other than for reasons of road safety on the petition of the police or local authorities, would merely delay a registration, it could not prevent it, yet the registration forms were boldly headed **Application** to register a local bus service.

As in all walks of life, the fear of change was principally in its anticipation, and once the new system was in operation the only difficulty arose from the actions of some operators trying to maintain or establish untenable positions. It was accurately forecast at the start that the deregulated system, designed to encourage new entrants to the field of bus operation, and as far as possible to set the existing operators at each others' throats, would eventually result in the re-amalgamation of the larger companies into two or three conglomerates like those which existed earlier in the history of the bus industry.

The Transport Act, 1930, introduced the road service licencing system to bring order to the earlier chaotic arrangements. The theory of the 1930 Act was admirable, but it failed lamentably in its objects. The small operators had been harassed by the large companies, and one of the purposes of the Act was to regulate licences to prevent this.

The managers of the large companies lived in the same sort of houses as the Traffic Commissioners, moved in the same social circle, attended the same functions, played at the same golf clubs, etc. It appeared all too often that the harassment of the small operators was now being aided and abetted by those appointed to regulate the industry. Alan Lambert's book 'Hants & Sussex', to which I referred in the North Downs chapter, shows this clearly.

It was demonstrated on one occasion before 1985, when I attended a Traffic Court hearing in which I was not involved. At the close of the proceedings the Chairman of the Commissioners invited the representatives of the County Council and the local National Bus Company subsidiary into the ante room for sherry, while the independent operators were left to disperse.

Traffic Commissioners are like judges, they are not often experts in bus operation in their own right, but rely on the evidence of expert witnesses. In the current situation of Operator licencing the evidence of vehicle examiners leads to objective decisions, but in road service licencing cases, the Commissioners had to adjudicate between the competing claims of applicants and objectors. It was often the superior power of argument and the knowledge and experience of how the system worked that won licences for the large companies, rather than the intrinsic merits of their case.

It was understandable that the small operators longed for an open system, but no system can protect small businesses from the predatory activities of large companies, whether it is in transport or paint manufacture. If small operators continue to exist, it is only by grace and favour of the large ones.

When the open system came, for political reasons, in 1986, the safeguards consisted of (a) the quality control of the Operator's Licence, administered by the Traffic Commissioners, and (b) the control of competition by the Office of Fair Trading. This simply means that if two operators wish to make any sort of a working agreement, the details must be registered with the O.F.T. In the event of a complaint, the operators can be required to cease the agreement. This is not so much to protect other operators as to protect the public from being 'taken for a ride' in the wrong sense by the parties to the agreement.

3. Taxibus.

The 1985 Act contained sections (11 & 12) which enable private hire cars to carry passengers sharing the vehicle and the cost for all or part of its journey, and allow licenced hackney carriages to operate registered local bus services.

As a result of the publicity given to these provisions, I was approached by two taxi operators in Berwick-upon-Tweed to help them set up a company, separate from their existing businesses, to operate taxibuses.

Certain principles were applied to the planning process. First, the vehicles must be immediately distinguishable from ordinary taxis. This could have been achieved by use of a distinctive colour scheme, but one of them said "We must have minibuses, because people will not get into a car with strangers".

Secondly, the schedule efficiency must be as high as possible. This meant as near as practicable continuous operation at as high an average speed as possible. To meet this requirement careful route and timetable planning were necessary.

Thirdly, the fares must be designed to produce the highest yield from a small number of passengers, i.e. it would be better to carry five people at 60p rather than six people at 50p. In general, fares would need to be comparable with bus fares rather than taxi rates, but a cheap fares policy to attract numbers of people would obviously be inappropriate for a taxibus.

It was decided to name the company Taxibus Services (Berwick) Ltd, and to use the largest vehicles able to be licenced as taxis - 8-seat minibuses. A 'minibus' is now legally defined as a vehicle with at least nine but not more than sixteen seats in addition to the driver, but the word is in colloquial use for any vehicle bigger than a car but not as big as a proper bus. Many bus operators refer to their 30-seat vehicles as minibuses.

The first disadvantage we faced was that vehicles with fewer than twelve seats including the driver were subject to taxes not applicable to larger vehicles. A new vehicle was subject to 10% Car Tax, on top of which went non-recoverable V.A.T., so a vehicle such as a Ford Transit, which could be bought as a 12-seater, cost 25% more if it had to be reduced to eight seats to enable it to be licenced as a taxi. Once on the road, its fares were (and still are) subject to V.A.T., while fares on larger vehicles are not.

Despite these disadvantages, it was still felt desirable to operate taxibuses rather than p.s.v. minibuses. Although based on sound enough reasoning at the time, it proved to be a fatal mistake.

This taxibus operation was not at all what was envisaged when the legislation was drafted. It was clearly the intention simply to allow taxis to operate little local services at separate fares to places or at times that buses did not go, or to satisfy the demands of such small numbers of people that buses would be inappropriate.

I was again a pioneer. The taxibus services we set up were bus services in miniature, with taxi-like features built in, such as off-route diversions. They were operated by vehicles designed or adapted for the purpose, and they were 'dedicated', i.e. they were not just providing services at times when the vehicles were not required for some other activity.

This operation was the largest, possibly the only, dedicated taxibus service in Britain, designed and built from scratch taking advantage of this new legislation.

In 1991, the Transport and Road Research Laboratory published a report which purported to be a review of all taxibus services registered since deregulation (there could not have been any earlier ones, anyway). There was one omission. They somehow overlooked the largest and most significant. Could the compilers of a Government report have been so careless? Perhaps there was some compelling reason for the omission of which we are not aware.

The first practical step was the acquisition from Northumberland County Council by competitive tender, of a local bus service contract to provide services between Berwick and Wooler from 27th October 1986. The specification was for shopping services to Berwick from the Milfield, Branxton and Etal area, which for operational convenience was to be contracted to originate from

Wooler, clearly in anticipation of the contract being awarded to an operator with a Wooler depot.

The settlements are arranged in such a way that one route linking them all is very tortuous, and the journey would probably have taken more than an hour. Similarly, although the previous bus services (United Automobile Services Route 467) had carried miniscule numbers of passengers, one taxibus might not have been adequate for peaks of demand, such as market days just before public holidays, when everybody shops as though they are not going to have another opportunity for weeks.

The company offered a timetable dividing the settlements into two groups. The first service started from Wooler and ran direct via Milfield and Etal to Berwick, taking only 35 minutes. The second service started from Branxton and ran via Crookham, Ford, Etal and Shoresdean, taking 40 minutes. It was stated that if this pattern should prove inadequate it would be possible to split the second service into two parts (and this was done with effect from 23rd March 1987 in anticipation of seasonal growth). This became Route 267.

A second contract was won by competitive tender, to provide half-hourly services between Berwick and Spittal on weekday evenings and all day Sundays.

A commercial service was registered to operate between Spittal and Eyemouth every half hour, but consequent discussions with the Borders Regional Council resulted in the reduction of frequency between Berwick and Eyemouth to hourly, and the extension of the route in a loop from Eyemouth via Ayton, Reston, Coldingham and St Abbs, contracted under Section 91 of the Transport Act 1985 to operate on weekday evenings and all day Sundays.

The evening and Sunday services were thus wholly contracted. The daytime commercial services during the week, every half-hour between Berwick and Spittal, were operated in alternate hours by the Wooler contract bus and by the commercial bus, which went to St Abbs every two hours. This may sound complicated, but it actually worked very well provided there were no delays.

The contract number for the St Abbs services was 235, so we

used this as the route number for the whole route from Spittal to St Abbs, including the 'shorts' between Berwick and Spittal.

Deregulation came early to the Borders, because the timetable changes hinged on the school year. The contracted services to St Abbs were required to start on Monday 18th August 1986. We thought we would have a running-in period, so Route 235 was licenced to start on Saturday 16th August. The previous day we ran a few demonstration services in Berwick for civic dignitaries.

One of the key features of the taxibus services was that they would all serve the railway station. The approach road was marked out to indicate its function as the approach to the Borough Council's car park, formerly a railway goods yard, as well as to the railway station. The taxibus could turn at a point approximately opposite the car park access.

There was a local train from Berwick to Newcastle at 0700 on weekday mornings, the stock for which arrived soon after 0600, having left Heaton depot at some unearthly hour. One of the staff from the Divisional Manager's office at Newcastle took the trouble to travel to Berwick with the empty stock on the Saturday morning expressly for the purpose of preventing the first taxibus from entering the approach road.

We had supposed it to be a public road as far as the car park, but apparently the whole of the approach road is railway property, and the public only has 'running powers' to reach the car park. As our taxibuses were not going to and from the car park but merely going to and from the station for the purpose of conveying passengers, they were not welcome.

The Borough Council allowed us to turn in the car park for about three weeks, which was the length of time it took them to persuade the railway management that they were being exceedingly foolish. An agreement was drawn up which required us to pay £500 per year for the privilege of providing rail passengers with services to and from the station forecourt. The company paid it in 1986 and was never asked for it again.

Ford Transit No 23 and Mercedes No 27 at Berwick Station.

The trouble arose from the fact that the railway is a property owner as well as a public transport operator, and each function is administered apparently without consideration of the effect on the other. I use the present tense because I doubt whether the internal conflict has yet been resolved, despite the separation of the Train Operating Companies from Railtrack. Some stations such as Berwick are actually run by the T.O.C's, but I have heard of one (not in this part of the country) which has pursued the course of conflict between its two functions, by setting punitive charges for buses entering railway property. The same firm runs buses as well, but for them it is merely an internal transfer charge, of course.

In preparation for the operation of the services, careful consideration was given to the choice of vehicle.

The Ford Transit 12-seat minibus, which had been nearly ideal in 1969 for the start of the North Downs services (except for the inadequate headroom), had now been re-designed in such a way as to make it totally unsuitable for our purpose, so that this possibility had to be dismissed immediately. Good reports were coming in from the bus industry about the reliability of the Mercedes-Benz vehicles (mostly 508Ds) which had been entering service with some companies, including the comparatively local Tyne & Wear P.T.E. It was found that the smaller T1 model (307D) was designed like the earlier Transit, with the added benefits that the headroom in the Mercedes was adequate, and the entrance door was nearly so. We would have liked another few inches on the door, but it was a whole foot better than anything else of the sort available at the time.

As we required only eight seats, the 207D short wheelbase version was sufficient. This was identical to the 307D except for the length and the suspension, and used 185x14 tyres instead of 215x14, so the entrance step was slightly lower.

We would have liked to lease two of these, but were only allowed one by the leasing company. We were going to buy a cheap vehicle to act as a stand-by, so now we had to buy two such, one of which would become our Wooler contract bus. The 'spare' was often in use for duplication, as in the illustration.

Ford Transit No 23 and Bedford CF No 22 operating in tandem on route 267, showing the normal traffic density on this road.

These vehicles were a Bedford CF and a short wheelbase Ford Transit, both with petrol engines. We identified them by the Borough Council's Hackney Carriage licence numbers, 22 and 23.

The Mercedes 207D (27) was adapted for our purpose by Derwent Coachworks at York, with eight seats, a luggage area just inside the door, and a destination indicator. This used the mechanism which had earlier been in North Downs No 5, and was

Mercedes 207D swb No 27 at Berwick Station, with 22 & 23 behind.

originally purchased for one of the ORTA Commers which had the standard roof, in the hope that it could be retro-fitted. This is the one piece of hardware that links all the concerns with which I have been involved.

The colour of the vehicle as supplied was a very pleasant blue. There was an indentation on the sides which, as part of the conversion, was painted cream, as was the roof. This blue and cream colour scheme was applied to all the taxibuses with great success. It was instantly recognisable yet it involved no designing or special masking, following the features of the bodywork. All vehicles have some feature which can be used for the cream stripe, not all in the same place, but all conveying the same effect.

This Mercedes is still in service in 1998, having covered about a million miles. (Yes, I do mean **miles**, not kilometres). The original gearbox is still in use, but in another vehicle.

After the services had been operating for a few weeks, and we were encouraged to think that they might develop, we had the chance to purchase a pre-used Mercedes 307D van, about a year old. The conversion of this van by Derwent Coachworks was bolder, and included an electric folding door. The entrance step was lower and the vehicle became a favourite of the elderly passengers who formed a significant part of our clientele.

There were two drawbacks with the door. It was built into the body in such a way that it increased the wind resistance considerably. Also, it tended to flip open at out-of-town speeds - not much, but enough to create a cool draught of air all round the bus. This was welcome on hot summer days, but not so for most of the year. A saloon heater was fitted, which we did not use because it was like most bus heaters in blowing cool rather than warm air over people's feet.

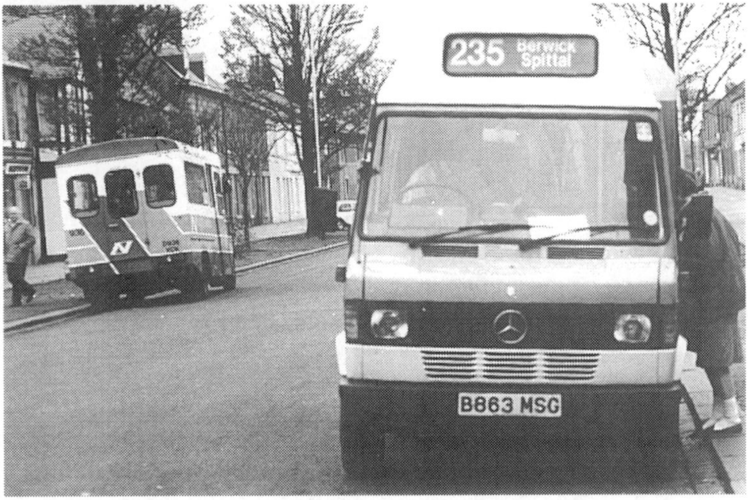

Mercedes 307D No 4 at Spittal, with a nearly-new Northumbria Motor Services 16-seat Sherpa across the road. This photograph was taken in 1987, about 17 years after the picture on page 71.

The coast in the Berwick area suffers from strong winds at times. One of our drivers had an unpleasant experience which could have been avoided with a moment's thought. He was driving along the 'mad mile' on the A1 north of Berwick in a very high wind. The bus was being buffeted so much that he thought he had a puncture, so he got out to have a look. One of the passengers thought that he would like to have a look, too, so he opened the emergency exit door at the back; the wind took it just as the driver came round the corner of the bus, and he took the full force of the door in the face.

One driver was known to have lower takings than average, and there were the usual whispers about why. When we investigated, he said it was because, although he **loved** the job - he really liked driving - he thought it was undignified to stop for passengers, so when he saw someone waiting he looked away and drove past. Shortly after that he became one of our ex-drivers.

Another driver had the foolish habit of issuing tickets before passengers had stated their destination or shown their travel pass. He was not alone in this. When I worked for London Transport I hopped on a bus which was nearing the end of its journey and the conductor rolled out a ticket for the fare to the terminus without noticing my staff pass, so he had to fill up a 'ticket issued in error' form. At least we were not very formal, and a note on the back of the waybill was enough, but he didn't learn.

From 23rd March 1987 the frequency of route 235 was increased to hourly, and from 11th May a new route 260 was introduced with some daytime services to Scremerston and evening services to Duns. Although registered as one route, with the same route number for both sections, they were only linked by the one service at 1910 from Scremerston which ran through to Duns.

The timetable for route 260 was dated to operate to 25th October 1987, but in fact it came to an abrupt end earlier as a result of some incorrect advice given to the company by its accountant.

As noted earlier, this work is intended as a readable record of the development of services and some of the vehicles used, taking a positive view of achievements. It does not become introspective about the financial problems. Those are for the students' supplement. Anybody who has been involved with a small business of any sort knows how difficult it is to achieve financial stability. One hears about the few who have been successful rather than the many who just survive, or fail to do even that. In the public transport business it is not usually possible to build on success quickly, or to correct mistakes immediately. Timetables have to be committed for long periods in advance, not because of the registration procedures but because of the inertia of the users, who cannot cope with frequent changes, especially in rural areas. Looking back at the dates of timetable changes, it is clear that they occurred much too frequently, but this was in a perpetual effort to reduce costs and maximise revenue.

One advantage of being a small operator is that the passengers know all the staff, including the decision-makers. In London Transport a good suggestion which, after consideration, had the full support of the managers, still took a very long time to implement. In our case, passengers knew they could have a word in the right ear and expect something to be done. I always knew when I had left it too long since doing some driving, because somebody would say something which showed that I did not know what was going on.

I was alarmed when a passenger said that she did not normally receive a ticket, and I tried to think who could be fiddling. Then I realised that on market days another independent operator with minibuses ran some services between Eyemouth and Berwick, and I believe it is true to say that they did not issue tickets. Of course drivers who have a mind to do so will fiddle a machine, but we certainly found that without the discipline of a ticket-machine, even if only self-imposed, drivers always paid in a lot less money.

In the south we had found that our news sheet 'North Downs News' had been a good way of telling our passengers what was going on, and we had some feed-back from them about what they thought. Our attempt to do the same thing here, 'Taxibus Talk', was a dismal failure.

To quell a possible back-bench revolt in 1985, the government gave operators an incentive to register rural bus services after deregulation, in the form of a transitional rural bus grant. This was 6p per mile for the first year, 5p for the second, 3.2p for the third, and 1p for the fourth year.

The Taxibus company's rural mileage was high, so the grant for the first two years was instrumental in keeping its head above water. The routes and services had mostly started from nothing, even route 267 being rather different from the bus route 467 which it had replaced.

Mercedes No 4 at Coldingham.

In 1988 the company burned its fingers badly by over-provision of services. The timetables were operationally efficient, but the cost of provision was far higher than even the peak summer season could sustain. Much effort was wasted on providing services which people did not require. While St Abbs and Coldingham people supported the taxibus services, there was very little interest at Reston, and virtually none at Ayton.

From 11th September 1988 there was a drastic pruning of mileage, deleting all commercial services to Ayton, Reston, Spittal, Norham, East Ord and Scremerston. The commercial effort was then concentrated on the route between Berwick and St Abbs.

In September 1988 a contract was won to replace a service discontinued by Northumbria Motor Services at 0730 from Alnwick to Berwick on Mondays to Fridays. This shocked them so much that they found that they were able to restore it in January 1989 so that the County Council could cancel the taxibus contract.

Towards the end of the contract period there was a very cold icy morning. My son Andrew was driving the taxibus to Alnwick, and after crossing the Lion Bridge there is a steep rise to the castle gate. He was almost at the top of this rise when he realised that he was not quite going to reach the top owing to loss of traction. The taxibus (No 4) started to slide back down the hill. Andrew had visions of going through the bridge parapet and dropping into the river, but at the foot of the hill there is a tree, under which the ice had not formed and there was a small area of dry road. One of the rear wheels held on the dry area, the bus pivoted about this wheel and came to rest on the bridge facing the way it had come.

On another occasion, and with a different driver, the same vehicle was approaching St Abbs on a similarly icy morning, when it slid across the road on a bend, turned round and rolled over the hedge into a field, coming to rest on its roof. Fortunately, as on the other occasion, this was a positioning service and there were no passengers, neither was the driver injured. We have been blessed throughout with resourceful mechanics, and on this occasion Alan Netherton came along with half a dozen old mattresses and rocked the bus gently until it rolled over onto its wheels. The only apparent damage was a broken mirror.

The Wooler route was now becoming less suitable for taxibus operation. Demand was concentrating onto a few services which were often inadequate while others were frequently almost empty.

From 9th January 1989 route 267 was transferred to B.P.C.Taxis, a partnership of two of our former drivers who fell out even before the transfer took effect. One of them struggled with it for more than a year, but the company took it back from 9th April 1990 and operated it jointly with new route 264, Berwick to Wooler via Lowick. It continued in this form until 15th April 1991, when a revised timetable for route 267 was introduced, built round some school contract services.

Throughout this period the two Mercedes (27 & 4) were the core of the operational fleet. The original Bedford and Transit were supplemented for the increased commitment in summer 1988 by another petrol Bedford CF, a Morris Marina car, and an ill-fated new diesel Transit (44). As noted earlier, the current Transit design is not at all suitable for bus work, and we suffered the usual delay in delivery of the diesel version, but its redeeming feature was its fuel economy. It was dangerously over-powered in the wrong hands, like most Transits, and this may have contributed to its early demise at the hands of a driver who allowed the rear to overtake the front in a lane. Fortunately again, there were no passengers involved.

The Marina car came from the family of one of the original taxi operators, and when the blue and cream colours were applied it was truly distinctive, becoming known as the Starsky & Hutch car. It worked as a duplicate to the buses on route 235 and became the mainstay of the evening and Sunday services to Norham (route 239).

When the Taxibus company started, the office was run by Anne Ray, who kept everybody's paper-work in order in the nicest possible way. She told me that my waybills were the untidiest. It was with great regret that we had to accept her resignation to take up another post. Our loss was the Co-op's gain.

We were fortunate that the closure of an old-established Berwick firm, William Elder's, in 1988 released Eddie Fairbairn, who came to us the following year. When he was on top of the paper-work he did some driving, and he was a first-class public-relations man and diplomatist. People would say things to him that they might not have felt quite comfortable about saying to me, and then Eddie would soften it a bit for me, and we got on fine.

In the autumn term 1991 route 264 was discontinued and most of the services on route 267 were taken over by Tweed Valley Coaches, a short-lived concern run by some ex-Lowland drivers based at Kelso. The very small remaining involvement in route 267 by the Taxibus company was brief, after which the company had no further part to play on this route.

The company had originally (1986) registered a half-hourly

frequency between Spittal and Eyemouth, which had been aborted before implementation as part of the agreement with the Borders Regional Council to extend the route to St Abbs. The summer 1988 timetable had pivoted around the interworking of routes 235 and 236 over the Berwick to Eyemouth section. The cessation of the Wooler services released resources so that a half-hourly frequency on route 235 between Berwick and St Abbs was introduced on 1st September 1991. The 'new' half of the frequency was reduced to Saturdays only from 27th December 1991 to 11th April 1992, and ceased again permanently at the end of the summer.

In 1990 another Mercedes 207D was acquired, so the three Mercedes met our requirements for the time being, but the following year a red Sherpa came into stock, to ensure that we had the ability to operate duplicates on route 235 in the summer. This was always necessary when the caravan sites, especially those at Coldingham, were busy.

The red Sherpa emerging from Railway Street.

The accumulated experience of taxibus operation led us to believe that fast, fairly long routes were the key to commercial success, and the short-hop round-the-town services were not, although a core supported service might offer the opportunity to build some commercial services around it, of course. We therefore turned our attention to using our existing route 235 as a springboard for a longer route.

For an experimental period, 28th November to 24th December 1992, two services per day with a 'late extra' on Saturdays and Sundays were operated from Berwick to Edinburgh (route 201). We expected to detect any potential for development in the course of this brief experiment.

I have hinted at the financial precariousness of the company, which was largely due to the burden of V.A.T. on fares and the natural ebb and flow of loadings, which meant that the need for duplication occurred much more quickly than it would have done with larger vehicles, when it would probably have been very rare.

Advice was received that we should 'let the company go down' and continue in a different form while setting up a p.s.v. operation. From the beginning of February 1993 the taxibus operations were taken over by myself trading as Cross-Country Connexions. Taxibus Services (Berwick) Ltd ceased trading, being wound up on the petition of H.M.Customs and Excise later in the year.

This photograph is a put-up job. It shows the vehicle which was used to provide the first taxibus service to St Abbs on Saturday 16th August 1986, No 27, driven by the same driver (the author), picking up the first passenger to travel on it, but taken ten years later, and showing the post-1993 Cross-Country ConneXions plaque on the door. In the meantime, the vehicle had covered nearly a million miles, almost all between Berwick and St Abbs. Unfortunately, the passenger was camera-shy and asked to be deleted from the published photograph.

4. Cross-Country Connexions.

From 29th March 1993 route 201 resumed operation with two services daily. From 8th August route 235 was amended slightly, and in reprinting the leaflet the fares on route 201 were made more user-friendly.

From 22nd September 1993 a new route 241 was introduced to replace services between Berwick and Roberts Lodge withdrawn by Northumbria Motor Services. Subsequently the route and service provision were altered in an attempt to achieve viability, first by diverting half of the services to run to and from East Ord.

Northumbria next withdrew services at school travel times from the Hiveacres estate, and Cross-Country Connexions' tender to replace them was successful. There followed a staged reduction in the commercial mileage operated to Roberts Lodge and East Ord to the point where virtually everything was contracted. The final withdrawal from East Ord came when the County Council diverted the resource to Scremerston to replace another Northumbria service.

Our next big break came when Lowland Omnibuses Ltd de-registered all of its services between Berwick and Dunbar except those required for the conveyance of schoolchildren to and from Eyemouth, and the balancing workings. Following normal local authority practice, the same operator was contracted to continue until the annual change of timetable in the summer.

Observers will have noticed that local authorities rarely take any initiative in connection with rural bus services. When an operator gives up a commercial service, their reaction is simply to continue the same service under contract, with apparently little consideration of the reason for its discontinuance as a commercial service. When Lowland de-registered their route 104, we found that the minimum size of vehicle the Council required to replace it was 25-seats. We enquired what was the maximum load on any vehicle at any time during the Council's survey of the route, and were told it was eight, but they would not consider replacement by smaller vehicles because one day there **might** be twelve walkers waiting for the bus.

The Council agreed that if we doubled the frequency of our Berwick - Edinburgh services it would not consider it necessary to let the contract for which tenders had been invited. It was our plan to become a p.s.v. operator, but we had to make haste slowly - much more slowly than the circumstances required, and at the date of the change, 31st July 1995, we were still operating only taxibuses. The Borders annual timetable revision is geared to school transport arrangements, which means that it occurs at the height of the tourist season. Our natural demand cycle was seasonal, so a change in the middle of the summer was very inconvenient for us.

It had been noticed that route number 201 was also used for a night route in Edinburgh, so the opportunity was taken to adopt the numbers 251 to 255 for our new group of routes, 201 becoming 251.

The new services were put under a great deal of pressure from the first day because of the holidaymakers. We suggested that the Council might consider contracting some additional capacity between Cockburnspath and Dunbar which could relieve us of the need to work via Innerwick. By the time they had let the contract the need had passed, but if they had contracted us to provide additional services quickly, we could have incorporated them into the general service pattern to everyone's advantage. Again they insisted on 25-seat vehicles, but observations reveal that the contracted services carry an average load of about three on a good day.

From 6th November 1995 the timetable was revised to interwork the Edinburgh services with route 235 between Berwick and Coldingham. This was an attempt to prepare again for a half-hourly frequency over this section, by patterning Route 251 etc to leave paths for additional services to Edinburgh, or Berwick to Coldingham 'shorts', which could be added seasonally.

During the 'high summer' period in 1996 an entirely new form of service was begun, utilising a Mercedes 240D car licenced as a Private Hire Car. Operated under Section 11 of the Transport Act 1985 as a Shared Hire Car service, it ran from Berwick to

Edinburgh via Chirnside and Duns to test the response. By its nature it only needed to operate if there were bookings. It was marketed as the Red Express Car Service. For the few weeks of the tourist season we offered it as a scenic excursion to Edinburgh through the Lammermuir hills, arriving at 1100, leaving at 1800, and conversely leaving Edinburgh for a scenic ride by the same route to Berwick for the afternoon, arriving back in Edinburgh at 1800. There was very little traffic, and from 2nd September it was revised to join our bus route at Grantshouse, and the afternoon times were advanced by one hour. Marketing during the winter began to produce results.

Since 1988 none of the vehicles operated as taxibuses had been owned by the company, but were rented. The demise of the Taxibus company therefore did not result in the loss of the vehicles, as they were not the company's property. The rental agreement was simply transferred to Cross-Country Connexions in February 1993, and for several years the stock of vehicles rented to the company, and subsequently C.C.Connexions, had been growing.

During 1996 the process of forming a company to be a p.s.v. operator had been going on. The company was registered as Cross-Country Connexions Ltd and the P.S.V. Operator's Licence was issued in December for ten vehicles, to allow for growth. An ounce of practical help is worth a pound of advice, and we had more than an ounce from Metrobus Ltd in enabling us to do this.

As always, financial stability had been a major problem during the t/a C.C.Cx period. The development of the Edinburgh services had been a strain on resources. When a new service begins, all the costs are incurred immediately and unremittingly, but while it is becoming established the revenue grows tantalisingly slowly.

The change to company operation, planned for 23rd March 1997, actually came into force in two stages. The first was on 23rd February, when the Berwick - Tweedmouth services under contract to Northumberland County Council were revised because of a change in Northumbria's town service timetables. The new contract was issued to the company from that date. At the same time new route 256, Berwick to Edinburgh via Duns, was begun by the company to replace the Red Express Car Service. The remainder of the services were taken over as planned on 23rd March.

The company took over well-established services, in consideration of which it settled the t/a Cross-Country Connexions outstanding accounts, other than to the Inland Revenue. To take this on would have placed it under a great strain, but it was certainly a bargain, because the other accounts to be settled were not enormous.

The normally helpful Fuel Duty Rebate section of the Department of Transport made the transfer to the company very difficult by altering the rules to which they had worked, to my knowledge, for thirty years. Small operators depend very much on the rebate, and we had become used to it being always totally reliable, to the penny and to the day. On this occasion somebody in the section dug himself into a pit and obdurately refused to discuss why he had changed long-standing rules. You cannot argue with civil servants. Once they have taken up a position it seems to be more than their life is worth to correct a mistake. They have to pretend that is how it was supposed to be, and then they change the rules again later to put things right. They also seem to think it doesn't matter when you receive your money so long as you get it sometime. I wonder if they would take the same view of a decision to delay their salary for a few months. Don't worry, old chap, you'll get it eventually. Our cash-flow went haywire as a result, and the planned smooth transition to the company was not smooth at all.

An offer of staged payment was made to the Inland Revenue, and if I had remained in charge of the company it would have been necessary to squeeze these payments out of revenue. This would have been difficult, but hopefully not impossible now that the Edinburgh services were established. The offer was not accepted, however, so the taxpayers at large have had to bear the loss, together with the not inconsiderable costs incurred. The company is now in new ownership, and free of that burden.

Epilogue.

Practically all the services described in this book were started from scratch. The only exceptions were the North Downs routes taken over from Mitchells and Brown Motor Services, the Taxibus route 267 which took over from a United bus route, and the Cross-Country Connexions routes locally in Berwick and from Berwick to Dunbar, taken over from Northumbria and Lowland respectively.

Hardly ever did these routes remain exactly in the form in which they were inherited. The route from Forest Green to Guildford, which became North Downs route 845, was probably the only one. Most were developed to make them more generally useful.

Many rural residents have enjoyed facilities as a result which they might not otherwise have had. Many, but not all, of the services begun, continued or adapted, are still being provided in some form. As mentioned in the North Downs chapter in connection with Ockley, rural people do not always take advantage of the facilities they have, and they may then lose them.

As a pioneer, I suffered from the fact that financial support by local authorities was virtually unknown during the ORTA and North Downs periods. In the later Taxibus era, the opportunities for contracted services were limited by the usual requirement for at least 25 seats. Such contracts as we had were therefore quite unusual, but needed to be linked with commercial services to make a viable network. The search for viability resulted in several false trails - when something new is begun, it has to be left for a while to develop before a judgement can be made as to its long-term value. It did seem as though the whole concept of taxibus operation was a false trail, compounded by the wretched V.A.T. element on the fares, adding injury to the insult of having only eight seats.

In retrospect, I can pick out the features of each concern which made it worth-while, and those which caused its problems. It is unfortunately never an option to be able to select all beneficial features and discard all difficulties, though that is what we all strive for. In the final analysis, is financial gain the only worthwhile criterion? I think not.

Carrying on where